SoundBlends

Quests and Dreams

SoundBlends

SoundBlends

Volume Three

Quests and Dreams

Erin Johnson

A **SoundBlendS** Book

Published by

Acadia Press

Copyright 2021 Acadia Press

SoundBlenders Volume Three: Quests and Dreams

ISBN# 978-0-9910458-2-2

Published by Acadia Press

Printed in the United States of America

Stories

What You Need to Know

Reading starts with Sounds...

Some of the English Sounds

Vowel Sounds

Consonant Sounds

What You Need to Know

Sounds and Letter Names are different

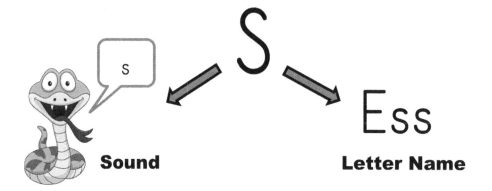

Sound　　　　　　　　　　　　　**Letter Name**

Letter Names help with Spelling NOT Reading

COW

Say: c + ow

Spell: See Oa Dubul-Yoo

The 26 Letter Names are shown in the section at the back of the book in More Information on **SoundBlendS**

What You Need to Know

Blend Sounds to say Words...

All 43 Vowel and Consonant Sounds as well as the spellings of these Sounds are shown in the More Information on **SoundBlends**... section at the back of the book

What You Need to Know

Blend Sounds to say Words...

All English Words can be made by blending the 43 Sounds

Blend 2 Sounds: c + ow → cow

Blend 3 Sounds: c + a + t → cat

Blend 4 Sounds: f + r + o + g → frog

Blending Consonant Sounds can be tricky!

What You Need to Know

The Reading Process:

Letters → Sounds → Words...

Simple Reading Process

1. See the Letters

2. Say the Sound

3. Blend the Sounds to say the Word

What You Need to Know

SoundBlendS makes reading easy...

Starting simple builds skills and confidence

- ➤ Story #1 uses only 8 simple Sounds
- ➤ Stories #1-5 use only 2 and 3 Sound Words
- ➤ The *most common* Sound for the Letters is taught first
- ➤ The Reading Process is the same for each and every Word throughout the stories

Story sequence progresses systematically

- ➤ Each story introduces new Sounds
- ➤ Stories and sentences become longer with more complex vocabulary
- ➤ Text font size gradually decreases

SoundBlendS builds confident readers!

What You Need to Know

SoundBlendS makes reading easy by...

Using font changes as visual cues

Black Font for Single Letter Sounds

Big dog dug.

Light Gray Font for Letter Groups = 1 Sound

Josh had fresh milk in a glass.

| Letter | Letter | Sight | Letter |
| Group | Group | Word | Group |

Dark Gray Font for the few Sight Words

Visual cues make it easy to read each and every word in these stories.

How to Go Through this Book

See the Letters

Say the Sounds

Blend the Sounds to

say Words

Say the Sounds

Start each Story by Saying the Sounds...

Sounds

a	A	c	C
t	T	s	S
f	F	h	H
	N		
i	o	u	b
d	g	m	p

Point at each Letter

Say the Sound

a

Blend Sounds to Make Words

Blend Sounds to say Words...

Words

c a t

h o t

s a t

Say each Sound

Blend Sounds to say Words

Read the Story

Blend Sounds to say Words...

Sam Cat sat.

Blend Sounds to say Words

Read the Story!

Letter Groups and Sight Words

Seeing Letter Groups...

Sound

Letter groups are used for 1 Sound

Light gray font with tight spacing

Sight Words use a Bold Gray Font...

to a of the was I are

The very few Sight Words are shown in a special font

Dark gray bold font with tight spacing

Words with Syllables

Syllables use Chunks of Blended Sounds

Extra Space between Chunks

ca mel

First blend the Chunks

ca = c + a

mel = m + e + l

Combine the Chunks to make the Word!

Split Letter Groups

Seeing Split Letter Groups...

Split Letter groups are used for 1 Sound

Light gray font with an under loop to connect the two letters

Hints:

- Split letter groups are the hardest to see
- There are no "silent letters"
- Letters can work together to represent 1 sound

SoundChangers

Letters or letter groups can represent more than 1 sound!

Font clues can help!

y = ie   y = y   y = ee

My yard is sunny.

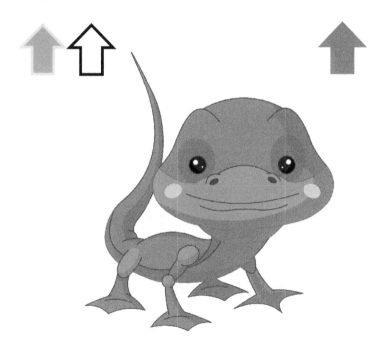

Sounds and Letters in this Book

Hint: Don't use letter names! Use the sounds!

Vowel Sounds

a	as in	**a**n = **a** + n
e	as in	**e**gg = **e** + gg
i	as in	**i**n = **i** + n
o, al	as in	**o**ff = **o** + ff
u	as in	**u**p = **u** + p
ay, ai, a_e, eigh	as in	s**ay** = s + **ay**
ee, ee, ey, y	as in	s**ee** = s + **ee**
ie, igh, i_e, y, eye	as in	s**igh** = s + **igh**
oa, oe, o_e	as in	**oa**k = **oa** + k
ur, ir, er, urr	as in	s**ir** = s + **ir**
oy, oi	as in	t**oy** = t + **oy**
ow, ou	as in	c**ow** = c + **ow**
ar	as in	c**ar** = c + **ar**
ew, ue, oo	as in	c**oo** = c + **oo**
aw, ough	as in	j**aw** = j + **aw**
oul	as in	c**oul**d = c + **oul** + d
are, air, err	as in	**air** = **air**
you, u_e	as in	**you** = **you**

Sounds and Letters in this Book

Hint: Don't use letter names! Use the sounds!

Consonant Sounds

b, B, bb	as in **b**ed	s, S, ss, se	as in **s**it
c, C, cc, k, K, ck	as in **c**at	t, T, tt, ed	as in **t**an
d, D, dd, ed	as in **d**og	v, V, ve	as in **v**an
f, F, ff, ph	as in **f**og	w, W, wh	as in **w**in
g, G, gg	as in **g**orilla	x, X	as in fo**x**
h, H	as in **h**at	y, Y	as in **y**ell
j, J, dg, dge, ge	as in **j**et	z, Z, zz, ze	as in **z**ip
l, L, ll	as in **l**id	th, Th	as in **th**at
m, M, mm	as in **m**an	sh, Sh	as in **sh**ip
n, N, nn, gn, kn	as in **n**od	ch, Ch, tch	as in **ch**ip
p, P, pp	as in **p**an	ng	as in si**ng**
r, R	as in **r**at	qu	as in **qu**ilt
le, tle	as in cas**tle**		

Sight Words

A   a   I   of   to   the   was   are   one   two

The SoundBlendS Pals

Horse presents...

The Seashore

Sounds

or   ore   our   oor

ar   oy   oi   igh   ie   ow   ou

ue   oo   ew   ur   ir   er   urr

oa   oe   ee   ea   ai   ay

a   e   i   o   u

th   tch   ch   sh   wh   ng

b   bb   c   cc   ck   d   dd   f   ff

g   gg   h   j   k   l   ll   m   mm

n   nn   p   pp   r   s   ss   se

t   tt   v   ve   w   x   z   zz   ze

Words

f or   a d ore s

y our   fl oor

m or n i ng   s ea sh ore

f our t ee n   d oor

or   n or th

p or ch   or c a

c or n   st or k

st ore   e x pl ore

a   to   I   of   the   was   are

Before Jan gets up, her dad is packing the car. It is Thursday morning. Jan and her dad are leaving for the seashore today. Jan's dad has rented a cabin next to the beach to stay for a long weekend. It is summer now and hot. But at the seashore, the cool breezes and the wet beach sand are fun to play in.

When Jan's dad finishes his packing, Jan gets up. Jan goes out to the kitchen to eat. Jan's mom is fixing eggs and cutting up peaches on a cutting board. Jan's twin sisters, Megan and Ora, are sitting in high chairs, waiting to eat. The twins are fourteen months and Jan adores them.

Megan cries out and reaches for Jan. Jan hugs her sister and Megan stops yelling. Ora ignores her sister Jan and plays with **the** peaches on her tray. Mom is staying with **the** twins this weekend. Jan will get **to** spend **the** weekend with just her dad.

Jan's dad had given her this trip as a birthday gift last May. Jan can not wait. After hugging Megan, Jan gets out a fork and a dish and sets them on the counter. Then Jan grabs a glass out of the cabinet and sets it down on the counter, too.

After that, Jan sits on a stool next to her dad. Jan's dad flashes a grin at her. Reaching across the counter, her dad lifts up a dish loaded with eggs and toast and sets it down in front of himself. Her dad turns and tells her, "This is a wonderful morning for a trip to the shore.

The forecast is clear for this weekend. Not a drop of rain in sight." Jan cheers and hugs her dad. Jan's mom asks her, "How about your eggs and peaches now?" Jan turns to her mom and grins, "Sounds fantastic." Jan's mom scoops the eggs onto

Jan's dish and Jan picks up her fork. Jan's dad pours her a glass of milk. Then, Jan's dad pours himself a cup of coffee and adds milk to it. Jan's dad sips his coffee as Jan eats her eggs and peaches. When Jan finishes eating, her mom asks, "More peaches or eggs, Jan?"

Jan tells her mom, "It was wonderful, Mom, but I had a lot to eat." Then Jan turns to her dad and tells him, "I can't wait to get to the shore. Let's leave, now, dad." Jan's dad grins at her, "First, finish your chores and then get your shorts and shirt on.

After that, pack a bag of sand toys to play with at the shore." Jan goes to finish her chores. Jan brushes her teeth, cleans her room, sweeps the floor, and feeds the cat and dog. Then Jan picks out a red shirt and blue shorts and gets them on.

Jan slips flip-flops on her feet and packs a beach bag with her toys. Jan goes out and hugs her mom and sisters before getting in her dad's car. Her dad leaves the house, starts the car and gets on the freeway. The cabin at the seashore is far away.

It is four hours north of Jan's house. On the way, the freeway skirts a charming fishing port. Jan can see four fishing boats and three crabbing boats tied up at the port. Lots of boats are missing as it is fishing season up north in Alaska.

Jan enjoys eating crab and fish. **To** pass **the** hours away, Jan's dad starts **to** sing. Her dad is singing **a** song that Jan adores, "This Land is Your Land." Jan joins him. Jan enjoys singing, too. Jan and her dad pass **a** corral with four horses.

Jan enjoys horses, too. Jan sighs and tells her dad, "I wish that I had a horse, Dad." Her dad grins and tells her, "I can see that." After three hours, Jan's dad sees that the car needs gas. Jan's dad gets off the freeway to fill up the car with gas.

Jan gets out to stretch her legs and goes into the store. In the store, Jan gets a bag of peanuts, a sport drink for herself and a cup of coffee for her dad. When Jan gets back to the car, her dad finishes pumping the gas. Jan and her dad get back in the car and set off for the cabin.

When Jan's dad gets off the freeway, it is not far to the cabin. The cabin is in a forest of fir trees. Jan's dad parks his car next to the cabin and Jan gets out. Jan goes up on the porch and waits for her dad to unlock the cabin. Her dad unlocks the door and goes in.

The cabin is charming and right next to the beach. When Jan goes in, her dad tells her, "The bedrooms are on the right. Unpack your bags and I will unpack the car. Then, how about exploring the beach?" Jan grins and tells him, "Sounds fun, dad." Jan goes and unpacks her bag.

Her room is painted a bright blue. Jan feels glad. The room is perfect. After unpacking, Jan sees her dad in the kitchen unloading the food into the cabinets. Her dad turns to Jan, grins, and tells her, "This is the last of it. Let's explore!"

Jan goes out onto the back porch and her dad locks the cabin door. The beach is right next to the back porch steps. Jan turns to her dad and asks, "Which way, dad?" Jan's dad sees a shed in the back and tells Jan, "Let's check out the boat house, first." Jan grins and tells him, "Boats are cool, Dad.

Let's check it out." Jan skips off **to the** boat house and goes in. In **the** shed is **a** boat with oars. Jan grins, "This is cool, dad. How about fishing in it this afternoon?" Jan's dad tells her, "Not now. **The** fishing is better in **the** morning." Jan grins, "**The** morning sounds fantastic, Dad."

Then, Jan skips off **to** **the** beach. Jan kicks off her flip-flops and runs in **the** wet sand. Jan feels **the** wet sand ooze between her toes. **The** roar **of** **the** surf is loud as it pounds **the** rocks off-shore. A fresh breeze drops sea mist onto her cheeks. Jan sees **a** crab scamper across **the** sand.

It dashes into a pool under a rock. Jan grabs a long stick and digs into the sand at the bottom of the pool. The crab snaps his pinchers at the stick and it cracks. Jan grins. Jan tosses the stick into the pool and goes down the beach.

Jan bends down and picks up a bright blue sea shell and tucks it into her pocket. Jan's dad taps her on her back and points north to a big gray rock. On the rock is a big bird with a gray pouch under its bill and brown wing tips. The bird flaps its wings, snatches a fish out of the sea and soars off.

Jan asks her dad, "Which bird is that? Is it a stork?" Jan's dad turns to her and explains, "That is a brown pelican. The stork's habitat is far away in Florida. Pelicans are different. See that pouch under its bill? It catches fish in it."

Jan grins and tells her dad, "Such a cool bird, dad." Just past the big rock, Jan sees a black fin appear in the sea. Jan points at it and asks her dad, "Dad is that a shark?" Jan is afraid of sharks and the fin frightens her. Jan's dad turns to see the fin in the sea.

It is a black dorsal fin, but it is bigger than a shark's fin. Her dad frowns, "That's not a shark's fin. Shark fins are gray. That is an orca fin. It is not common to see an orca this near to the shore." Just then, four other orcas appear around the rock. Now Jan is glad. Jan adores orcas.

51

This is her first real sighting of them swimming in the sea. Jan runs up the beach to the big rock and clambers up to the top of it. On top of the rock, Jan can see the orcas better. Jan dad gets out her camera and shoots the rest of her film. The orcas swim fast and disappear into the sea.

Jan jumps up and down and cheers, "Dad that was fantastic. I can't wait to tell Mom." Jan's dad grins at her, "Yes, that was fantastic. I got a lot of snapshots of the orcas. I think that your mom will enjoy seeing them." Jan tells her dad, "I am starving. Is it lunch, yet?"

Jan's dad grins and tells her, "Yes, it is way past lunch. How about grilling out on the back porch?" Jan tells her dad, "That sounds fantastic. Can I help?" Jan's dad tells her to get the corn out of the kitchen and shuck it. Jan goes into the kitchen, gets out the corn and peels the husks off of three cobs.

Jan's dad gets out the pork chops and sets them on the grill. Jan covers the corn with foil and sets them on the grill. The smells are wonderful. Jan can't wait until the corn and pork chops finish grilling. Jan sets up the dishes, forks and napkins and then goes to sit on a bench.

Her dad flips the pork chops and turns the corn with his long grilling tongs. Turning to Jan, her dad asks, "This is a fantastic way to start a holiday, isn't it?" Jan gets up and goes to hug her dad, "Dad, this is the best."

The End

The SoundBlendS Pal

Dragon presents ...

Dawn the Dragon

Sounds

aw   au   ough   augh

or   ore   our   oor   ar   oy   oi

igh   ie   ow   ou   ue   oo   ew

ur   ir   er   urr   oa   oe   ee   ea

ai   ay

a   **e**   **i**   **o**   **u**

th   tch   ch   sh   wh   ng

b   bb   **c**   cc   ck   **d**   **f**   ff

g   gg   **h**   **j**   **k**   **l**   ll   **m**   mm

n   nn   **p**   pp   **r**   **s**   ss   se

t   tt   **v**   **w**   **x**   **z**   zz   ze

Words

cl aw s   y aw n

th ough t   c augh t

l au n ch es   d au b s

d augh t e r   f au l t

ough t   s aw

th ough t f u l   f ough t

d i s tr augh t   l aw n

s tr aw   t augh t

a   to   I   of   the   was   are

Dawn is a dragon. Her skin is bright green. Her claws are red. Her wings are blue with silver. Dawn has a nest up high on a hill. It lets her see far across the land to the shore and past that to the deep blue sea in the west.

It lets her see **the** surf as it crashes onto **the** rocks causing spray **to** burst up and into **the** air. And it lets her see **the** farms and houses that dot **the** green land **to the** north, **the** east and **to the** south. On **a** bright August morning, Dawn gets up and out **of** her bed **of** rocks and straw.

Dawn starts **to** yawn and stretch her wings. It is **a** bright and clear summer day. Rays **of** morning sunlight stream down in**to** her lair, heating her up, which feels terrific. Yesterday, Dawn had thought that it might rain **to**day, but it **was** clear this morning.

65

Dawn grins, or at least tries to grin. It is hard for dragons to give a true grin. Dragons are big grouches. For a dragon, Dawn is cheerful and sweet. Dawn tends to grin when the sun is bright and hot and after a fresh filling meal. On other days, Dawn can act gruff or curt.

But that is not today. Today is a wonderful day. A terrific day. A fantastic day. Dawn stretches her wings and plans out her day. Is it better to soar to the sea or sun herself on a rock? Dawn considers her plans for the day. Then, Dawn goes out and sees the town under her hill.

The town is afraid of dragons. Now Dawn is not interested in bothering them. But, Dawn did not tell them that. As **the** farmers thought that Dawn might hurt them, each Tuesday morning **a** farmer ties up **a** cow, **a** sheep or **a** goat for her **to** eat. Dawn did not have **to** hunt or fret about getting food.

The farmers' fear keeps her fed and lets her enjoy herself. Hunting is hard. It is not fun **to** miss **a** meal. This way, her meals **are** effortless **to** get. Dawn thought that it **was** rather clever. On that bright August morning, Dawn stretches, thinks and is glad that **the** farmers in **the** town keep far away.

Just as Dawn lets out a loud yawn, a girl runs out of her front door and onto the lawn. The girl has tears streaming down her cheeks. Dawn can see that the girl is sad. Dawn gets caught up in the girl's sadness and starts to feel sad, too. The girl sits down on her soft grass lawn, sobbing deep sobs.

Dawn thinks to herself, "I ought to help that girl. If I flew down, might I help or might I frighten her too much?" Dawn chooses to help. Dawn launches herself off her hill and into a light breeze. Soaring with majestic poise, Dawn flies down to the girl.

Dawn lands with a soft thump on the green grass lawn next to the girl. The girl sees the dragon land, frightening her and causing her to start screaming for help. But, before the girl lets out a loud scream, Dawn tells her, "Girl, fear not. I saw your tears when I was high up on the hill.

I flew down to see if I might help with your problem." The girl catches her scream and stops the tears. The girl daubs her tears off her cheeks with a soft cloth. Then, the girl tells the dragon, "I lost a doll. It was a gift that Dad brought back after his long trip to the East. Dad bought it from a doll store.

It has a red dress, a blue shawl, and long black hair. I adore it. It is missing and I am sad." Dawn hears the girl tell about the doll and feels sad, too. Dawn thinks about the dad bringing back a doll for his daughter. The man was thoughtful to remember his daughter during such a long trip!

As Dawn thinks, **the** girl lets out **a** loud sniff and tries not **to** appear sad.   Just then, **a** boy sees **the** dragon next **to the** girl.   The boy sees **the** dragon's sharp red claws and feels fear.   The dragon had never visited **the** town before.   **The** boy's first thought is that **the** dragon might start hurting **the** girl.

The boy runs away screaming for help. The boy goes to tell the farmers and storekeepers about the dragon attack. The farmers bring pitchforks and dogs. A big strong storekeeper brings a saw and a hoe. Another storekeeper brings a long sharp stick.

The town had not fought a dragon in a hundred years. A man shouts at the dragon, "Flee now, dragon, or the fight will start now. I brought a long sharp stick and Joe brought his hoe. I understand how to fight dragons. I was taught when I was a kid living in Dragon Fighting Town."

Dawn feels upset. Dawn feels distraught. Dawn thinks that **the** town ought **to** wait and ask her about her visit, not start **to** attack her. Before **the** dragon replies, **the** girl stands up and tells **the** crowd, "The dragon is not attacking us. The dragon is helping. I lost a doll and **was** sad.

The dragon saw the tears and flew down to help." A murmur goes around the crowd. A man frowns, steps in front of the crowd and turns to speak to the dragon, "It is not your fault that this girl lost her doll. I am glad for your help. I had thought that dragons are mean and cruel.

I am glad to see that I was not right." With that, the crowd begins to clap. Dawn feels much better. Just then, a man runs up the road. It is the girl's dad. The man runs and hugs his daughter and tells her, "I can get another doll."

The dragon sees **the** dad hug his daughter. Dawn can see how much **the** dad adores his daughter. Dawn feels glad. Dawn turns **to the** crowd and tells them, "I am not mean. I am not cruel. I just wish **to** help this girl **to** uncover her lost doll."

With that, the crowd nods and goes back into the town. However, the man and his daughter stay. The girl grins at the dragon and tells her, "It is better now that the town understands that dragons will not burn it down or frighten the kids and adults.

I was taught that dragons are wicked and cruel. I was taught that dragons enjoy frightening girls and boys. I had a teacher tell our class about a fight between Sir Black and a wicked dragon, Smaug. The dragon, Smaug, had eaten his cows.

Sir Black had sought out the dragon in his lair and fought it until it died. During the fight, Sir Black was hurt and just about died. Sir Black had to crawl back to town as the dragon had cut up his right leg and left arm. Is this true?"

Dawn remembers the dragon, Smaug. Smaug was a bad dragon, cruel to men and other dragons, too. Dawn was not sad to see him beaten. But, Dawn did not tell the girl that. Dawn tells the girl, "It is true, but each dragon is different.

I am not mean or cruel. I enjoy helping not hurting. I will not fight or burn down this town. I ought to get back now." The girl nods and asks Dawn, "May I visit your nest high up on the hill?" Dawn thinks for a bit and then nods, "Yes."

The girl grins and hugs **the** dragon's neck. **The** dragon feels **a** tear spill on**to** her cheek. Dawn daubs up **the** tear with **the** tip **of** her wing. As **the** girl steps back, Dawn launches herself into flight. Soaring up, Dawn catches a flash **of** red and blue next **to** **the** barn. Dawn goes **to** check it out.

Dawn lands next to the barn and sees that the flash of blue and red was the girl's lost doll. The girl sees that Dawn has landed next to the barn and runs to her. Dawn slips her claw under the doll's dress and hands it to the girl. The girl hugs her doll as Dawn launches herself up into the air.

Her wings flap, causing a breeze that lifts up **the** girl's long brown hair. Dawn soars off **to** her nest, sits down on **the** soft straw and thinks **to** herself, "It feels wonderful **to** help."

The End

The **SoundBlenders** Pal

Macaw presents ...

If I Could Run...

Vowel and Combo Sounds

oul

aw   au   ough   augh

or   ore   our   oor   ar

oy   oi   igh   ie   ow   ou

ue   oo   ew   ur   ir   er   urr

oa   oe   ee   ea

ai   ay

a   e   i   o   u

Consonant Sounds

ce   ge   dge   dg

th   tch   ch   sh   wh

ng

b   bb   c   cc   ck   d   dd

f   ff   g   gg   h   j

k   l   ll   m   mm   n   nn

p   pp   r   s   ss   se

t   tt   v   w   x

y   z   zz   ze

Words

c ou l d   b ou n ce

w ou l d   d a n ce

sh ou l d   f e n ce

c ou l d n't   f l ee ce

w ou l d n't   p ea ce

sh ou l d n't   p ou n ce

      p r a n ce

      s i n ce

      v oi ce

Words

l ar ge   b r i dge

g or ge   do dge

sa va ge   e dge

m er ge   lo dge

v oy a ge   he dge

t win ge   do dg es

ur ge   b r i dg es

a   to   I   of   the

was   are

Alex sits in his wheelchair and sees the kids in his class play on the playground. Alex wishes that his legs could jump, run and play with the other kids. When Alex was four, a large truck had hit his mom's van. Alex was hurt and went to the hospital. It was an awful day.

Alex got better but his legs did not. Alex got a wheelchair to help him get around. Now sitting in his wheelchair, Alex wishes that his legs could still run. The kids in his class are playing Frisbee soccer out on the lawn. His pal, George, is on the Red team. The other team, the Blue team, is winning.

Just then, George dodges around Ynez and launches the Frisbee into the net. His score ties it up. The Red team cheers. Alex sits at the edge of the lawn and sighs. Alex wishes that the kids would play with him. Alex thinks to himself, "If I could run..." Then, Alex begins to daydream.

The kids on the playground disappear, and Alex sees himself running. "If I could run," Alex tells himself, "I would catch that Frisbee and score four goals before the other team could score. I would run faster than the fastest kid ever. I would catch the Frisbee and leap into the goal.

The kids would cheer, and I would jump and scream. I would begin running and would run past the kids in the playground. I would run out of town. I would run and run and end up in Montana. In Montana, I would see sheep running away from a cowboy on a black horse.

I would run up and help the cowboy catch his sheep. Since I could run fast, I would run around the sheep and urge them to run into a fenced-in pen. I would shut the sheep in the pen and keep running. The cowboy would grin and say that I was the fastest runner in Montana.

I should stop and help the cowboy more. The cowboy was just about to trim the fleece off the sheep. I should help him, but I can't stop running. I would grin and run off down the road and past a large hedge. Birds would flush out of the hedge. The birds would have never seen such a fast runner before and I frighten them.

I should stop and tell **the** birds that I am not a savage predator, but I can't stop running. I run past **the** birds. I would run faster and faster and end up in Texas. In Texas, I would see **a** rancher rounding up his cows. **The** cows run away, but I run faster and catch up **to** them.

I would herd them into a corner of the fence and the rancher could catch up to us. The rancher would grin and say that I was the fastest runner in Texas. I should stop and help the rancher more, but I can't stop running. I would cheer and run off. I would run and run and end up near a long bridge.

The bridge spans a deep gorge. It is a long way down. I would have the urge to stop and glance down at the deep gorge. I should stop to see the gorge with the bright red rocks and a swift river at the bottom. But I couldn't stop running.

I would cross more bridges spanning deep canyons, but I couldn't stop running. I would run across the desert. I would see a desert fox pounce on a rabbit, but the rabbit would get away. The desert would seem wonderful, but I couldn't stay for too long.

At the edge of the desert, I would start to see banana trees with large leaves. I would run and run between the trees and end up in Honduras. In Honduras, I would see a macaw as it soars in the rainforest. The macaw is red with green tips on its wings.

I would run with the macaw, but its short wings could not keep up. The macaw would plop down on the branch of a banana tree. I would run faster and faster and merge into traffic on a freeway. A red sports car tries to pass, but I am faster than the car.

I should let the sports car pass, but I can't stop running fast, and I end up in Brazil. In Brazil, I would splash into the biggest river, the Amazon River. I would switch from running to swimming. I would swim faster and faster. I would pass a large barge on a voyage up the river.

It would seem sluggish, and I would dodge around the barge. I should stop and explore the Amazon rainforest, but I can't stop swimming. I would swim down the river and end up at the sea. I would start to swim across the Atlantic. I would see a seal playing on a rock.

The seal would ask if I would play with him. I would tell the seal that I couldn't play today, as I am swimming too fast. Then, I would see a man in a boat catching fish. The man would set his net out in the blue sea to catch sea bass. I am interested in how fishermen catch fish.

I should ask him about fishing. I should stop and ask him which way I should swim, but I can't stop swimming and I end up in Africa. The trees on the coast of Africa are thick and green. When I reach the coast, I switch back to running, and I run under the branches of the thick green trees.

I frighten birds as I run under the trees. I would prefer not to frighten them, but I am running too fast to tell them that. I would run across Africa, out of the trees into the grasslands. I should stop and explore that vast African grassland, but I can't stop running.

I would see four cheetahs in the long grass. I would ask them if I could hunt with them. The cheetahs would start to run, but I would run faster and faster. I would run past the cheetahs. I should stop and see the interesting African animals but I can't stop running.

I could run south or I could run north. I pick north, and I run faster and faster and end up in Spain. I see a man in a car with his daughter. I could ask him which way I should run, but I can't speak Spanish, and I run past him. I would end up in Norway. It is summer in Norway, and the sun is up day and night.

I would see a boy sitting on the porch of a hunting lodge, eating dried fish and slurping milk under the midnight sun. I should stop and ask if I could play with him, but I can't stop running. I run faster and faster and end up in Japan. It is night in Japan, and the streetlights brighten the streets.

In Japan, I would see the fastest train ever zooming across the land. I would run and run. I should let them think that the train is faster, but I can't. I pass the train and end up at the sea. I would start swimming in the sea. I would swim faster and faster.

I would see a sailfish skimming across the sea. It has a large dark blue fin on its back that helps it swim fast. The sailfish is the fastest fish in the sea. The sailfish tries to keep up, but I would pass the sailfish and end up on the shore in New Zealand. In New Zealand, I would see lots and lots of sheep.

The fleece on the sheep would seem soft, and I would see ranchers sheering the fleece off and gathering the wool. The sheep would stand still, and I would run past them. I see a jet as it flies up high past a cloud. It flies fast but I run faster and pass the jet. When I reach the sea, I would switch to swimming.

I would swim a long way and end up in Canada. I would get out of the sea and start running. I would leap up sheer cliffs and see hawks soaring in the wind. I should stop and explore Canada, but I can't stop running. I would pass elk, deer, raccoons, and beavers.

As I ran past him, a big beaver would slap his tail to tell his kits to get back in the pond. I would run south and end up back at the playground before the bell had rung." Alex grins. It is a fantastic trip that Alex dreams about. Alex stops daydreaming.

Alex sees **the** kids playing on **the** playground. It seems fun **to** play Frisbee soccer. Then, Alex understands that his real wish is just **to** play with **the** other kids. His dreams **of** running cheer him up, but Alex wishes **to** play real sports with real kids.

Alex tells himself, "I would enjoy running, but I can still play with the other kids." Alex wheels his chair out onto the blacktop and shouts at George to toss him the Frisbee. George tosses Alex the Frisbee. Alex wheels himself around a boy.

Then, Alex dodges past a girl with brown curls and tosses the Frisbee to a girl on George's team, Sue. Sue scores a goal. His team cheers, and Sue hugs Alex and tells him that his pass led to the winning goal. Alex hugs Sue, too. Alex grins and thinks to himself, "I may not run, but I can play."

The End

The **SoundBlenders** Pal

Gnat presents ...

Sir Black the Knight

Vowel and Combo Sounds

le   tle

oul   aw   au   ough   augh

or   ore   our   oor

ar   oy   oi

igh   ie   ow   ou

ue   oo   ew   ur   ir   er   urr

oa   oe   ee   ea

ai   ay

a   e   i   o   u

Consonant Sounds

kn   gn

ce   ge   dge   dg

th   tch   ch   sh   wh   ng

b   bb   c   cc   ck   d   dd

f   ff   g   gg   h   j

k   l   ll   m   mm   n   nn

p   pp   r   s   ss   se

t   tt   v   w   x

z   zz   ze

Words

ni bb le   cas tle

a pp le   th is tle

h or ri b le   wh is tle

p ur p le   hus tle

sa dd le   bris tle

can d le   bus tle

ea g le   jos tle

ca tt le   mum b le s

stru gg le

Words

kn igh t   gn a t

kn ew   gn a sh

kn o ck   gn aw

kn ee   gn a t c a tch er

kn ee l s   f ore i gn

kn a p s a ck   kn u ck le

kn i t   kn o t

a   to   I   of   the

was   are

In a land far, far away, a sad knight sits in a tower high up in his castle. Sir Black has hidden up in his tower to get away from his problems. His main problem is a wicked dragon, Smaug. The dragon has eaten his cattle and horses and is frightening the farmers.

His other problem is that the king wishes him to get rid of Smaug. Now, Sir Black would enjoy getting rid of Smaug, but the dragon is wicked and cruel, and Sir Black is afraid to fight him. Just then, Sir Black hears a cheerful whistle. It is his daughter, Caitlin.

Caitlin is playing under his tower with her pet poodle, Noodles. Sir Black leans out **of** his tower **to** see his daughter play. Caitlin is playing fetch with Noodles in **the** courtyard. Caitlin tosses **a** bright red apple across **the** courtyard, and Noodles runs off **to** fetch it.

Caitlin whistles and Noodles runs back to her. Caitlin rubs Noodles' back and gives him lots and lots of praise. Noodles is a wonderful dog. As Caitlin plays, a man gallops across the drawbridge and into the courtyard, mounted on a large black horse. The man has on a long purple cloak.

Sir Black ducks back into his tower to keep out of the man's sight. The man with the purple cloak is an envoy from the king. Sir Black knew that the king would not let him avoid getting rid of Smaug. The man with the purple cloak stops Caitlin and asks her if Sir Black is in the castle.

Caitlin tells him that Sir Black is up in **the** tower. Sir Black hears his daughter and groans. **The** man with **the** purple cloak goes into **the** castle and up **the** stairs **to** **the** room at **the** top **of** **the** tower. Then, Sir Black hears **the** sound **of** knuckles knocking on **the** door. Sir Black feels horrible. Sir Black feels awful.

Sir Black wishes that **the** man would just disappear. But wishing **a** problem away will not solve it. With **a** sad sigh, Sir Black turns **the** knob and lets **the** man in. When **the** man steps into **the** room, Sir Black can see that it is another knight, Sir George.

Sir George bows and starts speaking, "Greetings, Sir Black. I have a message from the king." With that, Sir George sits down on a bench and gets out a letter. Then, Sir George hands Sir Black the letter. On the letter is the king's royal purple stamp of an eagle in flight.

Sir Black can tell that this letter is bad news for him. Sir Black sits down, too, and reads **the** letter. In it, **the** king orders him **to** slay **the** horrible dragon, Smaug. When Sir Black finishes reading **the** letter, tears begin **to** drip down his cheeks. Sir Black mumbles **to** himself, "This is it.

I will die if I have **to** fight that wicked dragon." Sir George sees **the** tears and tells **the** other knight, "Sir Black, keep your chin up and have faith. It is not that bad. With Smaug out **of the** way, peace will emerge in our land. **The** kingdom will cheer, and **the** king will shower your castle with wonderful gifts."

Sir Black leans out of his tower and sees his daughter playing. His sweet daughter means a lot to him. And the dragon might hurt her, too. Sir Black tells himself, "If I can slay this dragon, then I would protect not just the kingdom but Caitlin. I have fought dragons before and won. I might win this fight, too.

Without a wicked dragon around, Caitlin would not have to live in fear." Sir Black chooses to fight and slay the dragon, Smaug. Sir Black goes to his room and packs a knapsack with food. Then, Sir Black goes to get his dragon spear. Long before, Sir Black had lived in Dragon Fighting Town.

And in that town lived the best fighting teacher, Master Windoo. Master Windoo had taught him the best ways to slay a dragon. The best spot to attack a dragon is a weak spot in his chest. If a knight could get under the dragon, the spear could cut into the soft spot in the dragon's skin and slay it.

Sir Black had fought little dragons before, just to practice. Just before his first fight, Master Windoo had given him his dragon spear. It was a wonderful spear for little dragons. But seeing it now, Sir Black could not see how this little spear would help.

With a large dragon, such as Smaug, it seems just about impossible. Sir Black tries to ignore that thought. Sir Black grabs his spear and knapsack and goes out to the courtyard. Sir Black sees a man leading a goat to the barn and asks him to bring his best horse. The man stops and turns around.

The man bows to Sir Black and tells him, "Sir Black, the dragon has eaten them. I can't bring a mount fit for a knight." Sir Black frowns, "I need a horse. Ask the storekeepers in town for a strong horse." The man bows, drops the goat off at the barn and runs off to town.

After an hour, **the** groom returns with **a** frail gelding. It is gray with scars on its back legs. It limps and can not trot or canter. **The** gelding swishes **a** gnat away with his thin tail. Then, **the** poor horse snatches **a** bit **of** grass and chews it with **the** few teeth it has left.

Sir Black groans and cries out, "Is this **the** best horse that **the** shopkeepers can offer **the** knight that protects this town. This is an insult!" **The** groom whispers, "This is **the** last **of** **the** horses. A foreign merchant staying at **the** inn had brought this horse **to** sell at **the** market on Saturday. This is it."

Sir Black needs a mount, but a nag such as this? How horrible! Sir Black is mad and tries not to gnash his teeth in resentment. But, the knight cools himself down and turns to the man and tells him, "Get a saddle on the nag. And hustle, as I need to leave this afternoon."

The man bows and runs off to the tack room and grabs a saddle. With speed, the groom gets his saddle on. Sir Black goes to get four dogs for his trip. Sir Black thinks that the beagles might help fight the dragon. Sir Black mounts the nag and sets off with the beagles.

As **the** knight crosses his drawbridge, **a** gnat flies next him. Sir Black tries **to** brush **the** gnat away. The gnat buzzes louder in his ear. A gnatcatcher, **a** blue-gray bird, flies up **to** him, snatches up **the** gnat and hits Sir Black on **the** chin with his wings. It hurt!

Sir Black goes out onto the road, rubbing his chin. Just then, rain starts to drizzle and gets Sir Black wet. Sir Black's thoughts are miserable, "This is not a wonderful start to this trip." The drizzle did not bother the beagles. The dogs seem glad to run after the knight.

The knight plods along the road, asking his horse for more speed. The nag ignores his plea and plods along the road, stopping to nibble at grass. The drizzle turns to a pouring rain, soaking Sir Black's knapsack. It is not a fun trip. At dusk, Sir Black stops under an oak tree.

Since the light is vanishing, Sir Black can not see well. Sir Black dismounts into a deep puddle and wets his pants up to his knees. Sir Black groans and thinks, "This is horrible. Now I will have to camp in wet gear." The knight ties up his horse to the oak tree.

Then, Sir Black gets out food for **the** animals and sets up his tent. Sir Black kneels down and crawls into his tent. Sir Black gets out his knapsack. In his knapsack is **a** chunk **of** dried beef. Sir Black gnaws **the** dried beef before **the** light goes away. Sir Black is exhausted and goes **to** sleep.

The next morning, Sir Black gets up, eats, and feeds his animals.   Then, Sir Black saddles up and mounts his horse.   Then, **the** crew sets off for **the** lair **of the** wicked dragon, Smaug. As Sir Black nears **the** dragon's lair, **the** ground is burnt and smells **of** rotten eggs.

Sir Black's nag shuffles along the road, now eating bits of thistle, as the dragon has fried the grass near his lair. The dragon's lair is up on a hill of gray rocks. Steam curls up from the rocks telling the knight that the dragon is in his lair. Sir Black is afraid.

Sir Black thinks to himself, "Well, I can't give up now. I had better finish this." With that, the knight tries to urge on his horse to the dragon's lair. His gray nag ignores Sir Black and keeps plodding along. Sir Black gets his spear and his dogs and sneaks up to the dragon's lair.

165

In his lair, the dragon is getting up and stretching. Smaug lifts up his chest, raises his large wings and yawns. It is an incredible sight! Sir Black grabs his spear and rushes at the dragon. Smaug sees Sir Black and starts to cackle, "Another knight that I can play with."

With a flick of his wing, Smaug hits Sir Black's arm. The knight stumbles and drops down. His arm is cut and bleeding. The beagles attack the dragon. But Smaug brushes them off as a man might brush off an annoying gnat. The dogs run away, leaving Sir Black to fight the dragon.

With a gnawing pain in his arm, Sir Black struggles to get up. The knight reaches for his spear to attack the dragon. Smaug cackles and snorts at the weak knight. Sir Black hurls the spear and hits the dragon's chest. It lands on the dragon's soft spot!

But, the dragon's skin is too thick and the spear can't get in deeper into his chest. With a flick of his claw, Smaug slashes Sir Black's leg. Sir Black cries out in pain. Just then, the gray nag plods in to help the struggling knight. The gray horse sees the poor knight sitting down, hurt.

Now Sir Black had thought that this horse was helpless, but the knight was incorrect. This horse was the last of the horses due to his fighting skills. The gelding had fought off this dragon before and knew how to defend himself.

With a swift kick, the gelding thrusts the spear deep into the dragon's chest. The dragon groans and tumbles onto the rocks. Sir Black gets up and goes to see the dragon. The dragon is still. Sir Black goes back to his horse and tells him, "Your kick settled this fight.

I was incorrect about your skills as a knight's steed. In fact, your kick was wonderful. Pardon this poor knight's thoughtlessness." The gray horse nuzzles the knight. Delighted, cheerful and glad, Sir Black crawls back into the saddle. It feels wonderful to live.

The End

The **SoundBlenders** Pal

Eagle presents ...

The Soccer Match

Vowel and Combo Sounds

al   ui

le   tle   oul

aw   au   ough   augh

or   ore   our   oor

ar   oy   oi   igh   ie   ow

ou   ue   oo   ew

ur   ir   er   urr   oa   oe

ee   ea   ai   ay

a   e   i   o   u

Consonant Sounds

ed = d   *ed* = t

kn   gn

ce   ge   dge   dg

th   tch   ch   sh   wh   ng

b   bb   c   cc   ck   d   dd

f   ff   g   gg   h   j

k   l   ll   m   mm   n   nn

p   pp   r   s   ss   se

t   tt   v   w   x

z   zz   ze

Words

all

talking

call

chalk

hall

walking

tallest

small

walk

fruit

juice

bruise

cruise

suit

pursuit

a   to   I   of   the

was   are

SoundChangers

ed = d   *ed* = t

hu gg ed   w al k *ed*

th r i ll ed   d r e ss *ed*

c all l ed   ho pp *ed*

g r i nn ed   s l i pp *ed*

t u gg ed

g r a bb ed

On Saturday morning, Tom hopped out of bed and got his soccer outfit on. This was it. This was the day of the big soccer match between his team, the Hawks, and the Rockets. Tom had trained all season for this important match. This would settle which team was the best for this soccer season. The winner would get the winner's cup. Tom tugged his purple socks up to his knees and slipped sandals on his feet.

Tom packed his soccer bag with his cleats and extra ball and went down the hall to the kitchen. In the kitchen, Tom's mom was fixing eggs and French toast. His dad was pouring coffee into a mug and talking with Tom's sister, Fran. Fran was pouring orange juice into a tall blue glass. Tom's mom chuckled when Tom entered all dressed in his soccer outfit. Tom's mom asked him, "Well, today is the big day.

Is your team all set to win?"
Tom grinned at his mom,
"Mom, I think the Hawks will
win today. Our coach tells us
that our team is all set. I
can't wait to play." Just then,
Tom got a call. It was Ken.
Ken was on his soccer team.
Ken asked if Tom could walk
with him to the soccer match,
Tom agreed and offered, "How
about meeting on the front
porch at ten?" Ken replied
that that sounded fantastic
and hung up.

Then, Tom sat down on the stool, and his mom gave him a dish with eggs and French toast. Tom got himself a tall glass and poured orange juice into it. Tom couldn't eat much with his high stress level about the match. After clearing his dishes, Tom went to get a sport drink out of the hall cabinet to pack in his soccer bag. After grabbing a bottle and stuffing it into his bag, Tom went to brush his teeth.

After finishing his teeth, Tom's mom called him back to the kitchen, "Your coach called last night and asked if I could send a bag of chalk powder to mark the edges of the goal boxes. The chalk is in the garden shed out back. How about getting it for her?" Tom nodded, "I'll get it," and went out back to get the chalk. The chalk was in a plastic bag next to the hoe. Tom grabbed the chalk and walked back to his room.

Tom packed the chalk in his soccer bag. Just then, Tom's dad called him, "Tom, Got a second? I am in the kitchen." Tom ran down the hall and found his dad in the kitchen. Tom's dad was finishing rinsing the dishes. Tom's dad dried his hands and gave Tom a big hug, "Tom, your mom, sister and I will sit in the bleachers to cheer for your team. I just saw Ken walking up. Get your stuff together and meet Ken."

Feeling eager to get walking, Tom sprinted down the hall to his room to get his soccer bag. Then, Tom ran to the door, turned the door knob and greeted Ken, "Ken, I need to finish packing a snack. Have a seat on the couch." Ken sat down and waited. Tom ran to the kitchen and grabbed three snack bars, a juice box, and another sports drink. Tom packed the snacks, juice and sports drink into his bag and ran out to see Ken.

Ken saw Tom and grinned, "Tom, let's hustle. The coach needs us to help set up." Tom and Ken left Tom's house and walked ten blocks. Coach Kim was just getting out of her car. Coach Kim had the nets for the goals. Tom and Ken ran up and asked to help. Coach Kim handed Ken a net and asked him to attach the net on the south goal. Coach Kim asked Tom if his mom had found the chalk.

Tom grinned, "Yes, I've got it." and got out the chalk. Coach Kim asked Tom to mark the edge of the goal boxes with the chalk. Tom got out the chalk and marked the ground next to the south goal box. Then, Tom went to mark the other goal box. The chalk helped the players see the goal box better. Then, Coach Kim went back to her car to get out four orange flags on long thin sticks.

Coach Kim asked Tom to plant each flag into the grass to mark the four corners. The soccer players had to keep the ball within the flags. If the ball went out, then the other team got the ball. Tom walked around, jamming each flag stick into its spot. The light breeze caused the orange flags to flap and sway. When Tom was planting the flags, Coach Kim went back to her car to grab a large bag of soccer balls.

Soon, all the rest of his team started to appear and help set up, too. Bill, the tallest boy on the team, got the other net set up. Another boy, Jim, helped him. Soon, the set-up was all finished, and the kids started to play with the soccer balls. Soccer is a fun sport. To score a goal, the players have to kick the ball into the other team's net. Each player can pass it or kick it with his or her feet. Hands are not allowed.

191

At the end of the match, the team with more goals wins. Tom enjoyed playing soccer a lot. As it neared noon, Coach Kim called the team together to talk to them. Coach Kim huddled with the team and handed out the starting spots. Coach Kim had the tallest boy, Bill, play goalkeeper. It was his job to block the balls from getting into the net. Tom got to play right wing. Tom was thrilled. It was his best spot as Tom enjoyed scoring goals.

Ken was glad to play left wing. A smaller boy, Raul, got to play in the middle. The smallest boy, Josh, got to defend the goal. After that, Coach Kim handed out all the other spots. Tom's team was all set and could not wait to start. The last thing that Coach Kim did was shout, "Let's play strong! Let's play smart! Let's win today!" All the boys cheered. At noon, the referee got out his whistle and blew it.

The soccer match had started. The Hawks had the ball first. Tom passed the ball to Ken. Ken tried to dodge around a large boy on the Rockets. But the large boy got the ball. Ken tried to get the ball back but the other team passed it down and scored. Tom felt awful. This was a horrible way to start. After kicking off, Ken started to dribble the ball down to the goal.

When another boy got near, Ken passed the ball across the grass to Tom. Tom kicked the ball at the goal but the other team's goalkeeper caught it and tossed it back. The other team dribbled the ball down to the goal and scored for a second point. Tom's team was feeling awful. This was not the plan. The referee blew his whistle for a rest and the team went to see Coach Kim. Coach Kim was frowning when the players reached her.

Coach Kim got down on a knee and drew the team around her. Then, Coach Kim started to whisper to keep the other team from hearing her. Coach Kim whispered, "Well, this is not our best start, but I still think that our team can win. Let's adjust the players a bit and see if that might help." All the players nodded, and Coach Kim whispered the new plan. When the referee blew his whistle to start, Tom's team was all set.

Tom's coach had planned to shut out the other team's fastest runner, and to kick the ball up the middle. Tom ran hard and wore himself out. The other players on his team ran hard, too. With the new plan, Tom's team kept the other team from scoring. However, his team still could not score. When the referee blew his whistle, Tom needed the rest. Tom's coach had him sit out.

During the third part of the match, the other team scored a third point. Tom's team felt horrible. Tom had thought that his team would win. Tom could not see how his team could win today. Three boys on Tom's team got mad and started shouting at the coach. Coach Kim asked them to sit and cool down before speaking with her. Coach Kim whispered into Tom's ear, "Tom, I am adjusting our plan.

I am having Bill sit out and I am having Len play goalkeeper. Keep attacking the goal. Aim for the corners and away from the goalkeeper." Tom grinned and nodded. Tom went to talk with Ken and together the boys planned the attack. When the referee blew his whistle to start, Tom and Ken got into the right spots. Fred kicked the ball to Ken, and Ken dribbled it down the middle.

After crossing to the left, Ken passed it to Tom on the right. Tom aimed for the upper corner of the net and kicked hard. The ball went in, scoring his team's first goal. All the Hawks cheered. It felt fantastic to get a point. The Rockets kicked-off, but the ball went out. The Hawks threw the ball in. Ken ran up and slid into the ball, knocking it out of the other player's reach. Tim ran up to assist and passed it to Tom.

Tom dribbled the ball across the grass and kicked it hard into the upper corner of the goal, scoring the team's second goal. Tom's mom, dad and sister cheered. Tom was glad that his team was catching up. The other team kicked off. Tim ran up and picked the ball off. Tim passed the ball to Tom. Tom dribbled the ball down and was about to kick a goal when a boy from the other team ran into Tom, knocking him down.

Tom hit the ground hard, hurting his arm. The referee blew the whistle and offered Tom a free shot at the goal for the hard hit. Tom tried to ignore the gnawing pain in his arm. Tom aimed for the bottom right corner and kicked hard, scoring his team's third goal. Tom's team cheered. After the goal, Tom's arm was hurting too much. Tom had to sit down. Tom's mom, dad and sister ran to him and asked him about his arm.

Tom tried to keep the tears away, but it was too painful. Tom's mom held him, and his dad called out into the stands for a doctor or nurse. Len's mom ran down, inspected Tom's arm, and got a medical kit out of her car. Len's mom got out a large gauze pad and a bottle of disinfectant to clean up the cut. Tom winced when Len's mom rubbed it too hard. Then, Len's mom set it in a sling.

Tom needed to get to a hospital soon. It seemed that his arm would need a cast. But Tom did not wish to leave just yet. Just then, Tim passed the ball to Ken. Ken dribbled the ball down to the net and kicked the ball into the upper corner scoring the team's fourth point. Tom let out a loud cheer. His team was winning. Tom was glad. Just then, the referee blew his whistle to end the match. Tom's team had won.

Tom's team shouted and cheered. It was a fantastic win. His arm hurt still, but Tom was delighted that his team had won the winner's cup.

The End

The SoundBlenders Pal

Turkey presents ...

Queen Jean's Request

Vowel and Combo Sounds

e = e   *e* = ee

qu   ey

al   ui   le   tle   oul

aw   au   ough   augh

or   ore   our   oor

ar   oy   oi   igh   ie   ow

ou   ue   oo   ew

ur   ir   er   urr   oa   oe

ee   ea   ai   ay

a   e   i   o   u

Consonant Sounds

ed   =   d   *ed* =   t

kn   gn

ce   ge   dge   dg

th   tch   ch   sh   wh   ng

b   bb   c   cc   ck   d   dd

f   ff   g   gg   h   j

k   l   ll   m   mm   n   nn

p   pp   r   s   ss   se

t   tt   v   w   x

z   zz   ze

Words

qu i ck   k ey

qu ee n   v a ll ey

qu i l t   t ur k ey

qu ai l   d o n k ey

qu i ll   ch i m n ey

qu i n ce   b ar l ey

s qu i n t   m o n k ey

s qu aw k

a   to   I   of   the

was   are   one

SoundChangers

e = e   *e* = ee

h e n	m *e*
b e n ch	w *e*
e dge	*e* qu a l
qu e s t	f *e* v er
s e n se	h *e*
f e n ce	sh *e*
s *e* c r e t	
e g r e t	
e v e n	

In a tower up high in her castle, Queen Jean was drawing. She enjoyed getting up and drawing first thing in the morning. Queen Jean is a bright blue macaw and queen of all the birds. On that Sunday morning, Queen Jean sat on a soft quilt and was drawing a sketch of a squid swimming in the sea. Queen Jean adored her visits to the sea and often drew sketches of sea animals.

215

High up in her tower in her castle, Queen Jean could see down into her valley, across **the** hills and just about all **the** way **to** **the** sea. **To** sketch her drawings, she would dip a quail quill into a pot of black ink. **The** ink would soak into the quill. Then, Queen Jean would draw with **the** ink-filled quill. Her thinnest quail quill would let out just **the** right amount **of** ink to draw **a** wonderful sketch.

Queen Jean thought that her thin quail quills could not be more perfect. But just as Queen Jean **was** finishing her sketch **of the** swimming squid, **the** tip **of the** quail quill snapped. Queen Jean **was** upset. This **was the** last **one** **of** her quail quills. Queen Jean squawked for Sir Duck. Sir Duck **was** a knight **of** Queen Jean's. Sir Duck flew up **the** stairs **of the** tower **to** see his queen. Queen Jean asked Sir Duck **to** sit with her on her soft quilt.

Sir Duck sat down and saw the wonderful sketch of the squid. Sir Duck turned to Queen Jean and quacked, "This is a fantastic sketch of a squid. I enjoy all of your sketches, but I think that this is the best one yet." Queen Jean grinned and squawked, "I enjoy drawing them. If I had a choice, I would draw all day." Then, Queen Jean frowned, "But I can't draw, now. I have a horrible problem. Sir Duck, I need help.

This morning, when I was drawing the squid, the tip of the quill snapped. It was the last one. I need more quills, but I can not leave the castle to get them. I have to stay and greet a visiting prince this afternoon. I am asking for a few knights to get them for me. The quail that I got this last batch of quills from is living up north in a nest under an oak tree. I need a team of fearless knights to travel north to get the quills.

It is not a simple trip. It is long and it goes across the hawk's valley. On the last trip, the knights that I sent ran into big problems with a hawk." The queen shuddered at the thought of the hawk. Sir Duck got up and bowed to his queen, "Queen Jean, your request is this humble knight's command. I will get together a fearless team of knights and we will bring back the quills."

Queen Jean got off her quilt and turned to Sir Duck, "Sir Duck, I wish to send presents to the quail. I will pack a bag of gifts for him and send them down to the courtyard in the morning. That is all." Sir Duck bowed and went to get packed for his quest. On the way to his room, Sir Duck saw three other knights, Red Robin, Sir Starling and Mister Turkey, sipping fruit juice and talking.

Sir Duck stopped and quacked, "Greetings, Red Robin, Sir Starling, Mister Turkey. The queen has requested that I seek out a new batch of quail quills for her drawing and I would ..." Before Sir Duck could finish, Red Robin interrupted, "Sir Duck, how can we help? We all wish to join your trip if that would be of help to the queen." Sir Duck grinned, "I would enjoy your help.

Let's pack up and meet in the courtyard in the morning." Sir Starling replied, "Sounds wonderful." With that, Sir Duck went off to his room to pack a bag. Sir Duck got out his key to his room. He jammed the key in the lock and turned it. With a twist of the key and a turn of the knob, Sir Duck unlocked his room and went in. He sat on his bed and sighed.

Sir Duck was glad that Red Robin, Sir Starling and Mister Turkey agreed to join him, but he was still a little upset about the possible problems on the trip. Sir Duck packed a knapsack and got himself all set for bed. The next day would call for a long day of walking and Sir Duck needed his rest. The next morning Sir Duck got up and finished packing.

Walking down to the courtyard, Sir Duck could hear the braying of a donkey in his stall and the hustle and bustle of the castle getting up for the day. Sir Duck met Red Robin in the castle courtyard. Red Robin had on his knapsack. Before leaving the castle, a small turkey ran out to deliver them a box with the gifts for the quail. Sir Duck packed the box in his knapsack and the knights left the courtyard.

Red Robin led the team of four knights out past the drawbridge and onto the road to the north. The knights walked out of town passing farmers and merchants walking into town to sell things at the market. A farmer walked past them leading three donkeys loaded with honey and fruit to sell at the castle. A farmer with a horse loaded with barley stopped the knights and asked which way it was to the grain merchant.

Sir Duck was glad to help out. He pointed to the highest chimney in the town and quacked to the farmer, "See that highest chimney on the left? Keep that chimney in sight and it will lead to the grain merchant." The farmer grinned and went on his way. It was a bright August morning and Sir Duck squinted to keep the sun out. Mister Turkey grinned and got out sunglasses for them. It was better with the sunglasses.

As the knights got farther away from town, Sir Duck, Red Robin, Sir Starling and Mister Turkey did not see a lot of travelers. Yesterday, a thundershower had poured rain, leaving the trail wet. The mud squished and oozed in between the birds' toes. But it was fun to be walking on this bright morning and Sir Duck started to whistle. Red Robin joined him, and the whistle turned into a song. The knights all enjoyed singing.

Soon, the sounds of a rushing stream caught Sir Duck's ears. Around a bend, the knights saw that the stream cut across the trail. The bridge must have gotten swept away. Sir Duck turned to the other knights and quacked, "I think that I can swim us across the stream. Hop on." Mister Turkey thought that he was too large to fit on Sir Duck's back. Red Robin and Sir Starling hopped on Sir Duck's back. Then, Sir Duck swam across the stream.

Mister Turkey did not swim as well as Sir Duck, but he did manage to get across the stream. On the far shore, Sir Duck landed on a patch of sand and tried to get out but could not. The sand was quicksand and Sir Duck began to sink. Sir Duck cried out as the quicksand sucked at his legs. His legs couldn't budge. He was stuck. Red Robin and Sir Starling gripped Sir Duck's back and tried to lift up the stuck knight.

Together the birds managed to get Sir Duck out of the quicksand and onto true ground. The quicksand had just about gotten them all! Sir Duck sprawled out on the grass panting. Red Robin plopped down next to him to rest. Sir Starling rested on the branch of an olive tree. Since Mister Turkey had not gotten stuck in the quicksand, he was much more rested. But, he was glad for the rest, too.

It was exhausting, swimming across the swift stream. After a small rest, Sir Duck turned to Red Robin and quacked, "I am glad that the quicksand did not get us." Red Robin nodded, got up and chirped, "Let's get walking. I wish to reach the quail before it gets dark." Sir Starling and Mister Turkey chirped agreement and the knights set off down the road. This part of the trail went into a forest.

It was cool under the trees and the knights began to sing a medley of songs. The medley had bits and parts of four fun songs. After an hour under the trees, the knights saw the hawk's valley. The trail dipped down out of the forest into a valley filled with wheat and barley. Sir Duck and Red Robin could see small shrubs and hedges in the valley but not a tree was in sight.

The quail's nest was across the valley at the bottom of a tall hill. A breeze picked up and blew at the wheat and barley stalks causing them to bend to the ground. The trail was marked well and the knights walked with quick steps to the hill far away. The wind helped to cool them down, as it was hot under the August sun. Soaring in the wind, a hawk spied the traveling knights. Hawks enjoy catching other birds.

Without a sound, the hawk flew at the birds walking across the grass. Just then, Sir Duck happened to glance up to see the hawk swooping down on Sir Starling. He quacked at Sir Starling to duck. Sir Starling ducked out of the hawk's reach, but he still fell and bruised his knee. Sir Duck was quick to grab out a squirt gun from his pack. Sir Duck had thought that a hawk might attack them.

The squirt gun was loaded with a foul smelling liquid that Sir Duck had bought from a skunk. Hawks detest skunk spray. Sir Duck shouted at the hawk, "Quit bothering us. Queen Jean has sent us on an important quest." Squeezing the gun, the liquid squirted out sticking to the wings of the hawk. The hawk screeched at the bird, mad that the knights had attacked him. The hawk tried to knock off the awful-smelling liquid but could not.

The hawk then flew off to the stream to get the stinking skunk liquid off. Each knight let out a sigh, glad that the hawk had left. Sir Duck quacked, "Let's hustle. I wish to get out of this valley before the hawk returns." Red Robin, Sir Starling and Mister Turkey, all agreed and the knights sprinted off down the trail. It was not long before Sir Duck spied the oak tree under which the quail lived.

The knights stopped near the quail's nest. The quail was just getting up from his nap. The quail stretched his wings. When the quail saw the four knights, he squealed with joy. He was glad to see them. The quail asked the knights to sit down and have a rest. He went to get orange juice, tea and crackers to offer to his visitors. Glad for the rest, the knights nestled into the soft nest.

The quail asked them, "How about a glass of fresh squeezed orange juice? It is a long trip from the castle." Sir Duck nodded, "Cool orange juice in a glass sounds fantastic right now. We had such a long, hard trip. It is wonderful just to relax for a bit." Then the quail poured the orange juice into four tall blue glasses and handed them to each of the worn-out knights. Then, he asked them, "How is the queen?"

Sir Duck quacked, "The queen is well and sends her greetings. Our visit today is to help the queen. Queen Jean adores your quills and requests more of them." The quail squeaked, "I would be glad to help the queen." The quail got up and pointed to his tail, "Grab these tail quills. But please be quick as it tends to hurt." Sir Duck grabbed three quills and set them in his knapsack. Sir Duck knew that the queen would be pleased to get the quills.

When the quail sat back down, Sir Duck quacked, "The queen will be pleased to get the quills. And she sent gifts. I will get them out now." Then Sir Duck got out the gift box and set it in front of the quail. The quail squealed and tore the ribbon off the box. In the box, the queen had packed a blue silk quilt and the ink drawing of the squid swimming in the sea. The quail gasped. The sketch was wonderful.

The quail squeaked, "Tell the queen that the gifts are fantastic. This drawing of the swimming squid is stunning." Sir Duck, Red Robin, Sir Starling and Mister Turkey, all grinned. It was thoughtful of the queen to send such wonderful gifts. The quail hung up the squid drawing on the wall next to his kitchen and set the quilt on his bed. Then, the quail chirped, "It is such a long trip back to the castle.

How about staying the night and leaving first thing in the morning? I have room." The birds thought that that was a fantastic plan. The next morning, the birds got up. The quail asked them, "How would a cup of tea with a little bit of honey and fresh muffins sound?" Red Robin perked up and chirped, "Yes. I enjoy honey in tea." Sir Starling agreed, "Muffins would be fantastic. I would enjoy a cup of tea as well."

Mister Turkey was not talkative in the morning but he did grin. Sir Duck helped the quail serve the cups of tea. The quail had set a pot to boil and Sir Duck had gotten out the cups and put a tea bag into each. When the pot had begun boiling, Sir Duck poured the hot liquid into the cups. The quail got out a pot of honey. Then, he handed Red Robin a spoon to scoop out the honey into his cup.

Then, the birds sat down and enjoyed sipping tea. After tea, the knights left for the castle to deliver the quills. The hawk did not bother them on the return trip and the knights avoided the quicksand. Sir Duck was glad when he saw the castle tower in the distance. It had seemed such a long trip to get the quills. The problems with the quicksand and the hawk still bothered him. But he was glad to be back.

After crossing the draw bridge, he ran up to the top of the tower. He delivered the three thin quail quills to a delighted queen.

The End

The **So**u**nd**B**lenders** Pal

Snake presents ...

The Bake Sale

Vowel and Combo Sounds

a‿e   eigh

y = y   *y* = ee

e = e   *e* = ee

qu   ey   al   ui   le   tle   oul

aw   au   ough   augh

or   ore   our   oor   ar   oy

oi   igh   ie   ow   ou

ue   oo   ew

ur   ir   er   urr   oa   oe

ee   ea   ai   ay

a   e   i   o   u

Consonant Sounds

ed   = d   *ed* = t

kn   gn

ce   ge   dge   dg

th   tch   ch   sh   wh   ng

b   bb   c   cc   ck   d   dd

f   ff   g   gg   h   j

k   l   ll   m   mm   n   nn

p   pp   r   s   ss   se

t   tt   v   w   x

z   zz   ze

Words

grade

tame

bake

mate

cane

cape

bike

eigh t

eigh th

n eigh b or

w eigh ed

eigh t ee n

w eigh t

n eigh ed

f r eigh t

a   to   I   of   the

was   are   one   two

SoundChangers

y = y   y = ee

yell	quickly
yawn	pretty
yes	softly
yonder	cloudy
yesterday	jelly
yet	lucky
yard	squeaky
your	sunny
yam	windy

Jane enjoyed her first grade class in Room Eight. Her teacher was fun and Jane got to play with Ashley and Kate after lunch. Jane enjoyed playing in the sand box and on the monkey bars. On Tuesday, the eighth of September, after a fantastic lunch of peanut butter and jelly sandwiches, Jane went out to play with Kate and Ashley. Kate asked the two girls if a game of freeze tag would be fun.

255

Jane thought that freeze tag would be fantastic. Ashley went to get a few more players and the girls played out on the grass next to a tall hedge. It was a fantastic Fall day; sunny, cool and not too windy. Lots of kids played dodge ball on the blacktop, and baseball out on the grass. The bell to end lunch came too quickly. When the bell had rung, Jane walked back to her classroom and sat down at her desk.

When the rest of her class had walked in, her teacher, Miss Ridge, got up in front of the class. She held up her hand to tell the class to stop talking. Her teacher was frowning and seemed upset. Jane was puzzled. The class had behaved well. It did not make sense that Miss Ridge should be unhappy. Then, Jane found out.

Jane's teacher had to tell them bad news, "Boys and girls, I am sad to say that we have a problem, and the zoo trip is off. Our class did not get the money needed to pay for the bus to take us." Jane felt sad and disappointed. Jane had enjoyed her visits to the zoo. Ken raised his hand, "How about carpooling to the zoo? That way we could all take the trip without having to pay for the bus."

His teacher replied, "Ken, that is a wonderful thought, but the zoo has a small parking lot. The zookeeper requested that our class take a bus to keep the car parking spots free for the other visitors." Jane sat and thought about it. If her class raised the money, then perhaps the class could still enjoy the zoo trip. Jane raised her hand. Her teacher nodded at her, "Yes, Jane?"

Jane gathered her thoughts and asked, "Can our class make up the money?" Jane's teacher paused and thought about it. Then, the teacher replied, "Yes, I think that would make it possible." The class cheered. Jane raised her hand and asked her class, "I think that our class should plan a bake sale. I think that it would be easy to raise the money we need to pay for the bus. I can take charge. How about it?"

Kate cheered and shouted, "That is a wonderful plan, Jane." All the kids in the class agreed. Jane was happy that the kids in her class thought that she had a helpful plan. Ashley added, "If our class sells things at lunch, we could get a lot of the other kids to help us out." The kids in the class nodded. The plan was to set up the bake sale at lunch on Thursday.

Ken made up a handout telling the kids in all the other classes about the bake sale. Ashley made banners for the food booths. Kate went to ask if her class could take up all the lunchroom on Thursday for the bake sale. Quinn went to order the food booths for Thursday morning. All the kids in Jane's class started helping with the bake sale. After the class bell had rung, Jane saw her mom standing next to the oak tree out front.

Jane asked her mom for help in setting up the bake sale. Jane and her mom walked down the street and went up the stairs to her apartment. Jane walked back to her room. Then, Jane set her backpack on her bed and went in the kitchen to get a snack. Jane's mom called her neighbor, Fritz. Fritz had a bake shop downtown. Jane's mom explained to Fritz about the zoo trip. Fritz was happy to help out.

He offered **to** bring **a** truck filled with muffins, cakes and fudge **to** **the** bake sale. When Kate reached her house, her dad asked about her day. When Kate's dad found out about **the** bake sale, he called Jane **to** tell her that his store had extra apples and peaches that **the** class could sell. Ken's mom called Jane and offered **to** make sandwiches.

Cortez's mom had a candy shop and she offered to bring bags of jelly beans and honey pops to sell at the bake sale. Jane was happy to have such terrific help in getting set up for the bake sale. On Thursday morning, Jane asked her teacher if she and the class could set up an hour before lunch. Jane's teacher agreed. The class went at eleven to set up the food booths. All the moms and dads from Jane's class came to help.

A man from the milk store delivered boxes and boxes of fresh milk. Jane went to pick up the boxes of milk, but the boxes weighed too much. Jane asked Ken's dad to pick it up for her. Ken's dad was glad to help. With all the food, Jane had to set up eight booths. The first booth had the muffins, cakes and fudge. The second booth had the apples and peaches. The third booth had milk, fresh squeezed orange juice, and fruit punch.

The fourth booth had sandwiches. The fifth booth had even more sandwiches. The sixth booth had hot dogs and hamburgers. The seventh booth had freeze pops and the eighth booth had the candy. More and more kids brought in food. It made Jane glad to see all the help and support her classmates had gotten for the bake sale.

Jane thought to herself that with this amount of food, her class would make the needed money for the trip to the zoo. At noon, the lunch bell started ringing. The kids from the other classes came out. All the kids had planned to get lunch at the bake sale to help out Jane's class. At the end of lunch, Jane counted up the money that her class had gotten from the bake sale.

She thought that it should be more than the class needed to pay for the bus to the zoo. When Jane's class went back to Room Eight after lunch, the teacher was pleased to tell them the results of the bake sale. The bake sale had made the money needed to pay for the bus and pay for gifts for the eighteen volunteers that had helped out at the bake sale. The kids cheered loudly.

The zoo trip was back on and the new plan was to visit it on Tuesday. When Tuesday came, the bus came into the parking lot. All eighteen kids in Jane's class got on the bus and went to the zoo. The zoo was not too far. The bus went down Highway Eighteen, past a fruit stand selling fresh squeezed orange juice and past a lumber mill cutting fir trees into long boards. Jane could see stacks and stacks of logs waiting to be cut into boards.

Not long after that, the bus had to stop just before a set of train tracks when a large, long freight train blocked the road. The train whistle was deep and loud. Several kids started to make whistle noises, but Miss Ridge asked them to stop. That many kids screaming loudly was hurting her ears. It wasn't long before the bus turned into the zoo parking lot. The kids walked out of the bus and met under the tall oak tree.

Jane's class had her teacher, Miss Ridge, and eight adults to walk with them. The zookeeper met them at the front gate. He greeted them and asked that the kids enjoy themselves but not run or frighten the zoo animals. In the zoo, Jane's class went to see the bird exhibit first. The birdhouse was large and had black nets up high to keep the birds from getting out. Jane enjoyed seeing the macaws and peacocks.

Kate and Ashley thought that the bird with the sweetest song was the black and red starling. Sue and Will each got a handful of wheat grain from the bird keeper to toss to the blue jays. Ken thought that the black loon was a duck at first, until the bird keeper informed him that loons are a little different. After the bird house, Jane's class went to visit the monkeys.

The monkey exhibit was indoors and was part of a rain forest habitat. It was hot and steamy with tall banana trees and bushy ferns. Monkeys swung from tree to tree, playing tag and chattering with each other. It was fun seeing the monkeys swing on the branches. Jane was amazed to see how fast the monkeys could swing from branch to branch. Two male Howler monkeys called to each other in loud howls.

One male monkey was black and the other was dark brown with a tan chest. The zookeeper tried to tell Jane's class that the Howler monkey is one of the loudest animals, but it was hard to hear her speak. Jane had to cover her ears to keep out the loud noises. Ken tried to make monkey calls. His teacher was not pleased and asked him to keep his voice down. Ken grinned but stopped calling out.

After the monkeys, Jane's class went to visit the rain forest snake exhibit. Jane saw a large Anaconda that was eighteen feet long. Anacondas can coil around a small animal to squeeze it before gulping it down. Jane thought the snakes seemed creepy. Jane's class walked out of the rain forest exhibit and down the path to the next exhibit. The next stop was the panther exhibit.

The big cats sat up in the trees on flat boards that the zookeepers had hung for them. The day was sunny and starting to get hot. Clearly, the panthers enjoyed napping in the cool shade. After the panthers, the kids got to see the pandas. The pandas sat and chewed on bamboo. Jane asked her teacher if it was true that pandas had just about died out.

279

Jane's teacher frowned and replied that pandas did not have lots of cubs and that made it difficult for them to prosper. Jane frowned too. It would sadden Jane if the pandas died out. Jane's teacher saw Jane's frown and asked her to speak with the zookeeper. A man in a brown shirt came out, and Jane asked about the pandas.

The man grinned and informed Jane that the in-zoo breeding was helping keep the pandas around. In fact, the female panda, Shee Shee, was expecting a cub in eight weeks. Jane grinned. She was happy to hear that the zoo was helping the pandas to live. The last part of the zoo was an exhibit on farm animals. It was a petting zoo and the kids could pet all the animals.

The petting zoo had pigs, geese, sheep and goats as well as cows and horses. Jane adored horses and asked to help brush the mud off a black horse. The zookeeper let Jane brush his fur. Jane could tell that the brushing made the horse feel wonderful. After the kids left the petting farm, Jane's teacher asked them all to clean hands in the bathrooms. After scrubbing her hands clean, Jane went to get lunch.

Jane had a peanut butter and jelly sandwich, an apple and a carton of milk. Jane sat on the grass next to Kate and Ashley. It was cool in the shade under the trees. After lunch, Jane's class got back on the bus. The trip back felt long. Jane missed the zoo and wished that her class could have stayed longer. The bus was hot and noisy. Jane played games with Kate and Ashley. Jane's first game was a card game called Fish For Eights.

Two boys next to Kate chatted about yesterday's base ball game between the Red Socks and the A's. It was not too long before the bus got back. Back in the classroom, each kid got his or her backpack on and left. Jane's mom was waiting to walk her back to the apartment. When Jane saw her mom she hugged her and started telling all about the trip. Jane's mom was happy that she had had such a fantastic trip.

The next day, the kids in Jane's class drew cards for the volunteers at the bake sale. On the cover of the card, Jane drew a sketch of a monkey swinging in a tree. In the card Jane printed:

I am grateful for your help at the bake sale. Your help made it possible for our class to visit the zoo. I had fun at the zoo.   – Jane.

All the other kids made cards, too. Jane colored in the monkey with a brown marker pen. She drew a tall banana tree and colored it green and brown. Then, she handed the card to her teacher, Miss Ridge. Jane was happy that the bake sale had happened. The zoo trip was the best trip ever.

The End

The **SoundBlenders** Pal

Cub presents ...

Mike's New Bike

Vowel and Combo Sounds

i_e   eye

y = ie   y = y   y = ee

e = e   e = ee

a_e   eigh   qu   ey   al   ui

aw   au   ough   augh   le   tle   oul

or   ore   our   oor   ar   oy

oi   igh   ie   ow   ou   ue   oo   ew

ur   ir   er   urr   oa   oe

ee   ea   ai   ay

a   e   i   o   u

Consonant Sounds

wr

ed = d   *ed* = t

kn   gn

ce   ge   dge   dg

th   tch   ch   sh   wh   ng

b   bb   c   cc   ck   d   dd

f   ff   g   gg   h   j

k   l   ll   m   mm   n   nn

p   pp   r   rr   s   ss   se

t   tt   v   w   x

z   zz   ze

Words

bikes   eye

like   eyes

smiled   eyelid

knife   wreath

kite   wrong

write   wrist

white   wreck

outside   wrestle

quite   write

a   to   I   of   the

was   are   one   two

SoundChangers

y = y   *y* = ee   *y* = ie

y e ll	qu i ck l*y*	s k*y*
y aw n	pre tt *y*	m*y*
y e s	s o f t l*y*	sh*y*
y o n d er	cl ou d *y*	t r*y*
y a k	je ll *y*	wh*y*
y e t	lu ck *y*	b*y*
y ar d	s qu ea k *y*	d r*y*
y our	su nn *y*	f l*y*
y a m	w i n d*y*	s p*y*

A week before Mike turned eight, he went shopping with his mom at a big store. Mike's mom had to get new dishes and a flower wreath for the door. Mike thought that it would be fun to shop with her. He would get to see all the cool toys and stuff that he would like to get for his birthday. While his mom was getting her towels, Mike asked her if he could scout out the toys by himself.

295

She knew that Mike was a responsible boy and would not bother anyone. She smiled, "Yes, but behave well. It will not take me too long to get the kitchen towels." Mike agreed to behave and skipped off to see the toys. On the way, Mike passed the bikes. A red off-road bike caught his eye. It had shocks on the front and back wheels and big fat tires.

Mike knew that this was the bike for him. After seeing this bike, the other toys seemed less interesting. He kept still and did not budge, waiting for his mom to arrive. Mike was eyeing the new red bike when his mom caught up to him. He grabbed her arm and shouted, "Mom, see that red bike up on the top rack? That is the bike that I would like for my birthday next week."

Mike's mom smiled, "Mike, that is a cool bike." Mike's mom glanced at the tag and frowned, "Mike, that bike is a bit expensive. Perhaps another gift would be better." Mike pleaded, "Mom, I am turning eight next week. That bike would make it the best birthday ever!" Mike's mom smiled, "I can see that, Honey. But remember that one might be too much."

Mike's mom had not promised it, but Mike kept wishing and wishing for that red bike. During the rest of the week, Mike kept talking about the red bike and trying to convince his mom and dad to get it. His mom and dad would smile and tell him that he would have to wait and see. Mike saw an advertisement in the mail with the red bike on the cover.

Mike cut off the cover and taped it on the kitchen wall, next to the fridge. Each morning, Mike pointed at the bike and pleaded with his dad to get it for him. His dad would smile, agree with Mike that bikes can be fun, but never promised it to him. At night in bed before shutting his eyes and falling to sleep, Mike would dream about the red bike.

Mike could see himself on a dirt trail at the park, jumping off a bump, flying across a ditch and landing with a thud. He could see himself sprinting down a hill, dodging rocks and skidding to a stop at the bottom. Mike fell asleep dreaming about that fantastic red bike. Even during class, Mike would daydream about that red bike.

On Tuesday, Mike's teacher, Miss George, asked him to tell the class about the state of Vermont. Mike thought and thought, but nothing was in his brain but that red bike. Mike just blurted out, "Vermont has red bikes." His teacher was not pleased and asked another boy about Vermont. On Thursday, his teacher asked him to write an interesting fact about cars.

Mike thought and thought, but he was still thinking just about bikes. Mike printed, "Cars are like bikes." His teacher frowned and asked him to write another fact that did not have bikes in it. At long last, Saturday morning came. It was Mike's eighth birthday. Mike did not think about the cake. He did not think about the games. He did not think about the gifts.

All Mike could think about was that terrific new red off-road bike. His mom blew up balloons and wrapped two small presents. His dad made the birthday cake, cheese cake with fudge frosting. His uncle brought fried chicken and a fruit pie. His sister made fresh squeezed orange juice. It was a wonderful birthday feast. Mike's pals, Jake, Lin and Raul came at noon.

Mike's dad lit the candles on the cake and started singing Happy Birthday. Everyone joined in. Mike blew out the candles and cut the cake with a long sharp knife. He served the cheese cake onto the plates, added whipped cream and topped it with a pinch of chopped nuts. He then handed them out. The boys ate the cake quickly and then it was time for the presents.

Jake gave Mike a cool truck. Raul gave Mike a kite shaped like a bird. Lin's gift was a toy castle with knights on horses. Mike enjoyed all his presents, but it was hard not to think about the bike. Mike's mom whispered to him that his present would arrive after the boys left. Mike felt a thrill run up his spine. Mike just knew that it had to be that red bike.

The boys played with the new toys until it was pick-up time. After the boys left, Mike turned to his mom and dad, "Mom, Dad, my birthday party was fantastic! I had such a wonderful time." His mom and his dad smiled and hugged him. Then Mike remembered that his mom had whispered to him that his present would arrive after the boys had left.

He kept wishing that his mom and dad had gotten that red bike for him. Then Mike asked, "Is it time for your present, now?" His dad smiled, "Mike, your present will arrive soon. We should have eaten real food before **the** cake. How about a bite **of** fried chicken or a sandwich while we **are** waiting?" Mike did not feel like waiting, but went **to** get a snack anyway.

In the kitchen, Mike asked his dad, "May I try Uncle Mark's chicken? The last time he made it, I thought it was fantastic." His dad smiled and served him a fried chicken thigh and a wedge of a crisp red apple. Mike got himself a glass of fresh squeezed orange juice and sat down to eat. After Mike finished eating, a neighbor knocked on the front door.

Mike's neighbor, Sue had a big box with her. Mike's dad lifted the box up and set it down in the kitchen. Mike smiled. It was the right size and shape. It had to contain a bike. Mike got out a knife and cut the side of the box. The side of the box fell and inside was a bike. Mike gasped. It was a red bike, but it was not the bike from the store. Mike wheeled the bike out.

It was the wrong bike. It was not new or an off-road bike. The red paint was chipped and dull. The bike had horrible training wheels. Mike could not ride on dirt trails with training wheels. The training wheels would get caught on the rocks. Mike felt a lump in his throat. Mike was sad and disappointed. Tears filled Mike's eyes. He did not wish to cry.

Before the tears could fall down his cheeks, Mike ran off to his room. Mike hid under the covers and sobbed. Down in the kitchen, Mike's mom and dad could not understand why he was upset. Mike's mom turned to his dad and asked, "Why is he upset? He talked about getting a bike all the time. Mike's dad frowned, "I will talk with him about it."

Mike's dad went upstairs and knocked on Mike's door. Mike was upset and did not hear his dad knocking. Mike's dad could hear him sobbing and went in his room. After sitting on his bed, Mike's dad asked him, "Mike, let's talk about it." Mike sat up. His eyes felt red and raw from the tears. Mike gulped for air and tried to settle down.

Mike whispered, his voice hoarse and dry, "Dad, that bike wasn't it. It wasn't the bike I saw at the store. It isn't new and it isn't an off-road bike." Mike's dad frowned, "But Mike, that bike costs too much. Your mom and I tried to get a bike just like it." Mike could feel tears in his eyes and sobbed, "And Dad, it has training wheels on it.

I can not ride on the dirt trails with training wheels." Mike's dad rubbed his back, "It's all right, Mike. It is not hard to take the training wheels off. I have a wrench that can easily take them off. I thought that it might help at first. How about checking it out? Let's take it outside, ride it around the block and see how it goes." Mike got up and wiped the tears from his eyes.

Mike nodded and his dad hugged him. Then, Mike and his dad walked down the stairs to get the bike. Mike wheeled the bike outside and onto the street. Mike tried not to think about the other bike. Mike got on the bike and tried to smile at his dad. His dad smiled back. Mike started off on his bike and went around the block. His dad waved at Mike.

The gears on the bike squeaked and the training wheels made horrible noises as Mike pedaled around the corner. Out of his dad's sight, Mike got off his bike and sat on the curb. Mike covered his eyes with his hands to block out the scratches and chips on the dull red bike. Mike felt horrible. Mike did not wish to disappoint his mom and dad, but this bike was the wrong one.

Sitting on the edge of a hard curb, Mike tried to think how to handle this. He thought and thought but could not think of a way out of this. A boy walked down the street dribbling a basketball. His name was Zack. He had black curly hair and large brown eyes. Zack went up to Mike and grinned, "That is such a cool bike. Is it new?" Mike thought that the boy was teasing him.

Frowning, Mike replied in a sad voice, "I got it as a birthday present today, but it is not new." The boy smiled, "Wow, that is wonderful. I wish I had a bike like that." Mike was perplexed and thought to himself, "How could any boy like my rusty bike? It is horrible." But Mike saw the joy in the other boy's eyes and offered, "How about a ride on it?"

The boy cheered, "I would really enjoy a ride on your bike." Zack got on the bike and made wide turns in the street. Grinning from ear to ear, Zack pedaled faster and faster down the street. With a hard brake, Zack skidded to a stop and flipped the bike around. Then Zack pedaled quickly and flew back up the street.

321

Seeing Zack having fun made Mike think of his bike in a different way. Perhaps the bike was not quite as bad as Mike had thought it was. Maybe the bike really could be a lot of fun. Mike saw the joy in Zack's smile. When Zack finished, he sat down next to Mike. Mike turned to Zack, "Was it fun?" Zack grinned, "It was the best ride that I have ever had."

Then Zack frowned, "Mom tells us kids that bikes cost too much. But one day, I will have a fantastic bike like that. And it will just be my bike, not one that I have to split with my sisters." His eyes sparkled as his frown turned into a smile, dreaming about having a bike like Mike's. Then Zack grabbed his basketball, "Well I have to get back. Mom is waiting for me."

And then he started walking back down the street, dribbling his basketball. Mike got up and got on his bike. He thought to himself, "If Zack could like this bike, maybe I can like it too." He started pedaling around the block. The wind brushed back his fine brown hair and kissed his cheeks. He peddled faster and the bike flew down the street.

Mike then thought, "When I ride quickly, it feels like flying!" He could feel what Zack had felt. He could see that this bike really **was** a lot **of** fun. It did not have **to** have bright red paint. And he could take off **the** training wheels. He could paint on top **of the** rusty spots. He could add grease **to the** wheels **to** fix **the** squeaks. Best **of** all, he could ride his bike and have **a** lot **of** fun.

By the time that Mike got back to his house, he had a bright smile and happy eyes. He got off his bike quickly and ran inside his house to see his mom and dad. "Mom, Dad. I did not see my bike in the right way. Now, I can see how cool it really is. This really is a fantastic birthday gift!" Mike hugged his mom and dad. It turned out to be a wonderful birthday after all.

The End

The SoundBlenders Pal

Owl presents ...

The Queen's Rose

Vowel and Combo Sounds

o‿e   e‿e

i‿e   eye

y = ie   y = y   y = ee

e = e   *e* = ee

a‿e   eigh   qu   ey   al   ui

aw   au   ough   augh   le   tle   oul

or   ore   our   oor   ar   oy   oi

igh   ie   ow   ou   ue   oo   ew

ur   ir   er   urr   oa   oe

ee   ea   ai   ay

a   e   i   o   u

Consonant Sounds

gu

ed　=　d　　　　*ed*　=　t

wr　　　　kn　　　　gn

ce　　　ge　　　dge　　　dg

th　　　tch　　　ch　　　sh　　　wh　　　ng

b　　bb　　c　　cc　　ck　　　d　　dd

f　　ff　　　g　　gg　　h　　j

k　　l　　ll　　m　　mm　　　n　　nn

p　　pp　　r　　rr　　s　　ss　　se

t　　tt　　　v　　w　　x

z　　zz　　　ze

Words

l o n e	gu ar d
r o s e	gu i l t
ch o k e	gu i d e
d o v e	gu i t ar
gn o m e	gu y
qu o t e	gu e s t
h e r e	th e s e
s e v e r e	e x t r e m e
c o m p l e t e	a th l e t e

a	to	I	of	the
was	are	one	two	

332

SoundChangers

o = o   o = oa

got   so
wrong   bold
cottage   cozy
knock   don't
office   hello
dolly   golden
pocket   no
song   open
holly   only

In a land, far, far away, in a castle up high on a hill, a lone girl was waiting for a wizard. Her name was Nicole, the queen's daughter. She was sitting on a soft bench, eyeing a small wren out in the garden. The blue wren was pecking at wriggling bugs in the soft mud. Nicole sighed and thought to herself that it would be so much simpler to be a bird.

335

At last, the wizard came out of the queen's room in his long white robes edged with golden stripes. The two guards outside the queen's door bowed to the wizard as he emerged. Nicole got up and asked the wizard, "Master Wizard, is the queen feeling better now?" The wizard frowned and replied, "Your Highness, the queen is not well. I am sad to say that I can not heal her this time."

Nicole felt tears well up in her eyes and her throat tighten. **The** distraught girl fought back her tears and cleared her throat. Then she asked, "Why is she so ill?" **The** Master Wizard seemed quite sad, "Your Highness, I can't tell why she is so ill. I am sad **to** say that this is quite beyond my skills. I have seen many illnesses but this **one** is a severe case. I can not even guess why she is so ill."

Saddened by the news, Nicole could only whisper, "I am grateful for your efforts, even if it did not heal her. May I see her, now?" The wizard paused and then nodded yes, "I don't think that a visit will hurt her. But keep it short. She is quite weak and needs to sleep." Nicole turned the brass knob to open the door and walked softly into the queen's room.

The queen lay on a soft bed covered with a white and purple goose down quilt. Nicole knelt next to the queen's bed and asked her, "My Queen Mother, how may I help?" The sick queen opened up her eyes to see her daughter and whispered in a hoarse voice, "Nicole, my darling daughter, I am not feeling well. The Master Wizard has tried all his spells but can not fix this wrong.

The only thing I can think of is to ask the wise owl. The wise owl lives not too far from here. He has a nest up high in an old elm tree deep in the Black Forest. Here take these two quills for luck. These can help. If problems arise, toss them both into the wind." The queen reached into her purse and brought out two quills. She handed them to Nicole. One quill was gold and the other one was silver.

Nicole had never seen anything like it before. She did not understand how **the** quills might help but she tucked them into her pocket anyway. With that, **the** queen closed her eyes and went **to** sleep. Nicole got up and wiped **the** tears from her eyes. **The** queen seemed so weak and frail. She **was** completely unlike **the** strong, confident queen that Nicole knew. Nicole went out **of the** queen's room and into **the** castle courtyard.

As she walked past the gardens, Nicole saw Guy, a brave knight. He knew the Black Forest well and might help guide her to the wise owl's elm tree. She told him, "Sir Guy, I need to take a trip to the Black Forest. Saddle up the horses as I need to set off this morning." Sir Guy was puzzled but replied, "Yes, Your Highness." Nicole went up to her room to pack her bags for a quick trip to the Black Forest.

Sir Guy brought out the horses. Nicole attached her bags to the saddle and mounted up. Then spurring the horses on, Nicole and Sir Guy galloped out of town. It was not far to the Black Forest and it was a delightful day for a ride. The sky was a bright blue and the light breeze was crisp without being cold. The horses became tired during the ride, but Nicole felt the need to get to the wise owl as quickly as possible.

At the edge of the forest, Nicole and Sir Guy passed near a quince tree, with ripe golden fruit just waiting to be plucked. Nicole adored quince and told Sir Guy, "Let's stop here for a rest. The horses are tired and I would like to pick a quince or two. Sir Guy agreed and got down off his horse. He tied both horses to a tree close to the stream that ran by the quince tree.

Dodging bees that buzzed around the quince tree, Nicole scrambled up the branches to reach the top part of the tree. She grabbed a large ripe quince and bit into it. Its juice was sweet and it dripped down her chin. She picked eight more and tossed them down to Sir Guy. Nicole thought that it was quite lucky to have stumbled upon this quince tree with its sweet and ripe fruit.

After a short stop, the two got back in the saddles and started into the forest. While it was a bright day, the shade from the trees blocked out the sunshine in the Black Forest. As the trail got smaller, Nicole and Sir Guy had to walk the horses. It was cooler in the forest. The trail grew faint and hard to see. Nicole was starting to fear that the trail might disappear.

Suddenly, after turning a bend, Nicole saw a man sitting on a rock strumming a guitar. It seemed odd that he would be here. Why would a man be playing out in the middle of a forest? She stopped her horse and asked the guitar player, "Pardon me sir, we are seeking the home of the wise owl. He lives in an old elm tree. Is it far?"

The guitar player stopped playing and his brown eyes lit up as he recognized the queen's daughter. He smiled, "Your Highness, I am honored. My name is Bard George and I have played my guitar for the queen and her court last summer. Yes, the wise owl is not too far from here. Just over the hill, past a white cottage and down to your left is his elm tree."

Nicole smiled, "Bard George, I am happy that it is not too far. Our horses are getting tired. Your guitar playing is delightful. After my quest is over, when I have more time, please stop by the castle and ask for me. I would enjoy listening to more." With that, Nicole urged her horse on down the trail. It was not long before Nicole saw the elm tree that the wise owl lived in.

Dismounting, Nicole called up to the owl, "Greetings, wise owl. I am in need of your assistance." An owl popped out of a big hole up high in the elm tree. Blinking his eyes the owl replied, "I am the wise owl. How may I help, queen's daughter?" Nicole was startled and whispered to Sir Guy, "How could the owl tell that I was the queen's daughter? I have never met him before."

The wise owl could hear the girl whispering and replied, "I am the wise owl. I knew about your trip long before now. A little wren was sitting in a castle garden during your talk with the queen. That wren flew here faster than your horses to report back to me. For me to be a wise owl, I need to understand everything that goes on in the kingdom." Nicole nodded, "Well then, may I ask how I can best help the queen to get better?"

The wise owl closed his eyes to think. Nicole and Sir Guy waited as the owl thought. Then, the wise owl opened his eyelids and sighed, "Your Highness, I am afraid that the news might be grim. The thing that can help the queen is far away and difficult to reach." Nicole gasped, "No matter how far or difficult, Sir Guy and I will get it. Just tell us how." The wise owl nodded, "All right.

It is a silver rose that is in the garden of the wicked witch of the west. A large and savage dragon stands guard over the garden and protects the rose from harm. But if the queen smells the rose, it will make her better." With that, the wise owl ducked back into his hole. Nicole turned to Sir Guy, "Let's get new horses and set off for the rose, now." Sir Guy frowned, "Your Highness, it might be better if I get it alone.

It is not safe in the wicked witch's garden. Dragons are difficult to deal with. The kingdom can not risk the queen's daughter on this task." Nicole nodded, "I understand, but I need to get that rose, myself. I need to help the queen. I can not sit around waiting. I will feel much better if I can help." Sir Guy frowned but nodded, "All right. Let's stop at the nearest inn and get fresh horses for the ride."

Nicole nodded and got on her saddle. Sir Guy set off down the trail. Before Nicole could ride away, the wise owl flew out of his hole in the tree. Landing on a branch near her, Nicole could see that the owl had a small golden bell in his beak. The wise owl hopped off the branch and dropped the bell into Nicole's hand. The owl whispered, "If times are difficult, ring this bell and help will arrive." With that, the owl flew off.

Nicole tucked the bell into her pocket next to the two quills and rode off to catch Sir Guy. Nicole and Sir Guy galloped to the nearest inn. The innkeeper knew Nicole and Sir Guy and let them trade horses. It was getting quite late and so Nicole thought that it would be best to lodge that night at the inn. The innkeeper's wife served them fresh stew. After dinner, his oldest daughter led them to the rooms.

The innkeeper and his wife had eight daughters, each of them as cheery and happy as the next. The next morning dawned fresh and bright. After a quick cup of coffee, a wedge of cheese and a quince from the tree in the Black Forest, Nicole and Sir Guy galloped off down the road. The fresh horses allowed Nicole and Sir Guy to ride quickly across the wide valley that led to the wicked witch's castle.

At the bottom of the valley, a large river gushed. The bridge that crossed the river was blocked by a small gnome. Nicole thought that it would be easy to get by the gnome. But he got out a wicked spear, pointed it at them and told them to stop. In a harsh voice, he shouted, "Stop, no one can pass this bridge without paying me the toll." Nicole was annoyed, "I am the queen's daughter.

I should be allowed **to** pass any bridge in the queen's land." Nicole tried **to** think **of** another way around **the** gnome. **The** river seemed too large **to** ride across. And she couldn't see any boats **to** take them across. She sighed. **The** gnome giggled, "Not so, Your Highness. Every **one** needs **to** pay **the** toll. In your case, I will be easy. Tell me **the** correct response **to** my riddle and I will grant your passage across this fine bridge."

Nicole groaned, "All right. Tell us the riddle." The gnome cackled, "I am wetter as I dry. I am a..." The gnome paused, waiting for Nicole to reply. Nicole did not get it. Nothing should be wetter when it is dry. Stumped, she turned to Sir Guy and asked him, "Sir Guy, any thoughts?" Sir Guy shrugged, "No, Your Highness. I can not say." The gnome cackled louder. He was happy that he had stumped them with his riddle.

Then, Nicole thought about the silver and gold quills that the queen had given her. She got them out of her pocket and tossed them into the wind. The quills did not fall. The two soared up into the sky and clinked together to make an extremely loud noise. Soon, two geese arrived. One was gold and the other was silver. The gold goose landed next to Nicole and bowed, "Your Highness.

My name is Aurum and her name is Arjen. We are here at your command." Getting over her shock at seeing two geese made of gold and silver, Nicole asked him, "The gnome will not let us pass unless we give the right response to his riddle: I am wetter as I dry. I am..." The silver goose snorted while the golden goose hooted. When the two stopped, the silver goose told her, "Why that is a towel of course!

A towel gets wet when it dries off anything!" As that was the correct response, the gnome stormed off, peeved that the geese had solved his riddle. Finished with the task, the two geese bowed and then flew off into the blue sky. Nicole waved to the geese, happy to be getting on her way. It was not long before Nicole and Sir Guy could see the witch's castle. It was up high on a hill. Her gardens lay in a valley south of the castle.

As Nicole and Sir Guy rode west, **the** land grew more and more bleak. **The** farmers would frown and scowl at them. Nicole tried not **to** let it bother her, but **the** queen's daughter saw parts **of** her kingdom that lived in fear. Nicole vowed **to** rid this land **of** **the** wicked witch if possible. It **was** not right that **the** wicked witch could frighten her subjects this way. A mile east **of** **the** witch's gardens, Sir Guy stopped.

The knight turned to Nicole and asked, "Your Highness, this is the last spot to turn around. It is not safe in the wicked witch's garden and dragons are unpredictable." Nicole replied, "Sir Guy, I am getting that silver rose for the queen. Nothing is going to stop me. Let's ride." With that, Nicole rode down the road to the witch's garden and the awaiting dragon. The dragon was not difficult to spot.

He was extremely large with long blue wings and sharp spikes along his spine. He was perched upon a ridge over his lair. The grass was charred near the dragon's lair and steam curled up from the rocks around him. Sir Guy got out his dragon spear and rode up to the dragon. Sir Guy shouted at the dragon, "Dragon, let us pass to the witch's garden. The queen has need of a plant that the witch raises inside."

The dragon chuckled at the sight of the knight, "The witch has forbidden all to pass into the garden and that spear will not help. Go away." Nicole stepped up and addressed the dragon, "Noble Dragon, I need a rose that is inside the garden to help the queen. The queen is ill and needs a silver rose inside the garden to make her well." The dragon paused and peered at the girl.

After considering it, the dragon replied, "I regret that I can not help. The witch has commanded that the garden remain closed." Nicole peered at the dragon. The queen's daughter had enjoyed reading in her castle about dragons. Dragons tended to act cross and ill-tempered and preferred to keep to the northern parts of the kingdom. It was odd that this dragon would take orders from a witch.

Nicole stepped up to the dragon and asked, "It is odd that a dragon would take orders from a witch. How is the wicked witch keeping a fine dragon, such as yourself, to protect her garden?" The dragon frowned and grew sad. Then the dragon replied, "The witch has a little sister of mine locked up high in her tower. I need to protect the garden in order to keep her alive."

Nicole frowned and asked the dragon, "If we free your sister, can I get the rose from the garden?" The dragon rose up and unfurled his wings, "Yes, if Little Sister is freed, I will even help." Nicole nodded and went to talk with Sir Guy. Nicole whispered in his ear, "I think that our chances are better if we get the dragon's sister out of the witch's tower than to try and fight him.

Besides, it is not right that the witch is holding his sister captive." Sir Guy nodded, "I agree." Nicole and Sir Guy mounted the horses and set off for the wicked witch's castle. As Nicole and Sir Guy neared the castle, a band of guards surrounded them. Pointing spears at the knight and the queen's daughter, the guards herded them into the castle. The wicked witch met them inside the castle.

The witch let out an awful cackle, "This is a fantastic catch, men. Wonderful job. Take them to the tower for keeping." A man poked Nicole and Sir Guy with a spear, pointing at the stairs leading up to the top of the tower. Nicole feared that the witch would not treat them well. At the top of the stairs, Nicole could hear horrible noises, a whack and a thud that made the whole tower tremble.

The man prodding them gave a wicked cackle, "Will not last long in that room!" The man unlocked the door and hit Nicole on the back. Nicole stumbled into the room and Sir Guy ran in to help her. The wicked man slammed the door shut, locking them in. Inside the tower room, Nicole could see a small pale blue dragon flailing about, hitting the walls with her wings and tail.

The small dragon turned and scowled at Nicole and Sir Guy. The dragon was about to attack them when Nicole stepped up and shouted, "Wait, Don't attack us just yet! I met your brother down in the witch's garden. We would like to help with your escape." The dragon paused, stopping her attack. She started sobbing, large tears the size of grapefruit fell from her eyes.

Steam from her tears formed little clouds around her ears. Then the dragon spoke, "I was caught last spring. I just wish I could escape, but the witch has cast a spell on the tower and I can not get out." Then, Nicole remembered the little silver bell that the wise owl had given her. Getting it out of her pocket, Nicole let it ring. At first, the silver bell made a small sound. But then the sound grew higher and louder filling the tower.

The rocks began to rumble in the walls. The sound grew louder and louder. The rocks quivered, wobbled and started falling out. The top part of the tower fell out leaving a hole in the wall. It was a big hole. Nicole saw how to escape. Nicole ran to the dragon and told her, "Dragon, now is the time. Let us get on your back and fly out of this wicked castle."

The dragon smiled at the sight of the blue sky that she could see in the hole and agreed. Nicole and Sir Guy got on her back and the dragon unfurled her wings. With a leap, the dragon launched herself into the air. The wicked witch's men saw the dragon soar off and raised the alarm, but it was too late. The dragon flew to her brother and landed next to him. Nicole and Sir Guy went to the other dragon.

Nicole asked him, "May I have the rose, now." The dragon smiled, "Yes, feel free to take the silver rose." The dragon turned to his sister, "Little Sister, your escape is wonderful. Fly them back to the castle to help the queen. I need to go speak with the wicked witch about her horrible treatment of us." Then the dragon launched himself and flew to the wicked witch's castle.

Nicole was glad that the dragon was not letting the witch get away with her bad treatment of him and his sister. Then Nicole turned and went into the garden. The silver rose was near the gate and Nicole plucked a blossom. Then Nicole and Sir Guy got on Little Sister. Little Sister launched herself into the air and flew back to the queen's castle. Landing in the courtyard, Nicole and Sir Guy scrambled off.

Nicole turned to the dragon, "I am grateful for your help." Nicole gave the dragon a quick hug and then ran up to the queen's bedroom. Turning the brass knob and opening the door, Nicole went in the room. The sick queen still lay on her bed wrapped up in her purple and white quilt. Nicole set the rose under her nose. The queen drew in the fresh rose smell.

After breathing in ten times, the queen sat up, all better. Nicole was delighted. The rose had made the queen better. Nicole hugged her mother. The queen hugged her back. All was well. Soon after, Nicole and the queen went down into the courtyard. The big blue dragon and his little sister sat sunning themselves under the blue sky.

Nicole asked the big dragon about the wicked witch and the dragon replied, "I think that all are safe from her wickedness now." His satisfied grin told Nicole that he had gotten rid of the wicked witch. Nicole was glad that the kingdom was safe from the witch now and that the queen had recovered. It was a wonderful day.

The End

The **SoundBlenders** Pal

Bear Presents...

Summer Camp

Vowel and Combo Sounds

u‿e   you   are   ear   ere   eir

oo = oul   ow = oa   o = oa

y = ie   y = ee   e = ee

a‿e   o‿e   e‿e   i‿e   eye

eigh   qu   ey   al

aw   au   ough   augh   le   tle   oul

or   ore   our   oor   ar   oy   oi

igh   ie   ow   ou   ue   oo   ew   ui

ur   ir   er   urr   oa   oe

ee   ea   ai   ay

a   e   i   o   u

Consonant Sounds

ph

ed = d   *ed* = t

gu   wr   kn   gn

ce   ge   dge   dg

th   tch   ch   sh   wh   ng

b   bb   c   cc   ck   d   dd

f   ff   g   gg   h   j

k   l   ll   m   mm   n   nn

p   pp   r   rr   s   ss   se

t   tt   v   w   x   y

z   zz   ze

Words

cube   cute

perfume   amuse

use   excuse

volume   refuse

mute   mule

elephant   dolphin

photo   phoney

phone   trophy

sphere   orphan

graphic   phantom

Words

b are   c are f u l

s c are   s qu are

f l are   sh are

h are   s t are

b ear   p ear

w ear   t ear

wh ere   th ere

th eir   th eir s

a   to   I   of   the

was   are   one   two

SoundChangers

oo = oo   *oo* = oul

s oo n   b *oo* k

m oo se   r *oo* f

s n oo ze   t *oo* k

p oo d le   w *oo* d

z oo   s t *oo* d

oo ze   l *oo* k

ch oo se   s t *oo* d

g r oo ve   g *oo* d

r oo s t er   f *oo* t b all

390

SoundChangers

ow = ow	ow = oa
b r ow n	y e ll *ow*
c ow	sh *ow*
f l ow er	b l *ow*
sh ow er	b *ow* l
t ow n	p i ll *ow*
n ow	kn *ow*
ow l	th r *ow*
c l ow n	e l b *ow*
b ow	b *ow*

Yellow morning sunlight was streaming into Ralph's room when his alarm clock went off. Buzz. Buzz. Its volume was so loud that he hit the snooze bar hard, knocking the whole clock off his night stand. Ralph opened his eyes, grimaced and thought, "Well at least it stopped. I hope that the clock is okay." He bent down to pick up his clock. His dog, George, bounded into his room and leaped up onto his bed, settling on his pillow with a sigh.

Ralph rubbed his ears and whispered, "Good Morning, George. You are such a cute dog. You look like you are just as happy to see me as I am to see you." Ralph hugged him around his neck and then went to get out of his pajamas. He got on brown shorts and a white shirt. Ralph was both happy and sad. Happy that he was going to Camp Skyline this morning and sad that this was going to be his last day of camp.

He looked out the window. It looked like it was going to be a fantastic August day, sunny but not too hot. Just then, Ralph's mom called up the stairs, "Ralph, are you up, yet? It's time to eat. We have to leave soon." Ralph called down, "Be there in a flash, mom." He ran out of his room with George bounding after him. When he reached the staircase, Ralph grinned.

He thought that if there is an easy way and a fun way to go down the stairs, take the fun way. He slid down the railing and landed with a thud at the bottom. His mom was standing there, frowning. "Ralph, why don't you use the stairs like everyone else?" Ralph got up grinning, "Mom, I did use the best part of the stairs. The railing is perfect for a fast ride down."

His mom's lips curled up into a smile, "All right, then. You need to hurry and eat. We have to leave soon." "No problem, Mom. I can't wait to get to Camp Skyline. This is going to be the best day of the whole week. Our team is going to crush the other team and win the Grand Camp Challenge." At the beginning of the week, the campers had split up into two teams, the Phantom Bears and the Massive Elephants.

Each day, the two teams had competed in fun games. But today was going to be different. Today, the winners of the challenge would win the camp trophy. Each member of the winning team would get a camping kit, filled with useful things like a pocket knife or a carving knife. With thoughts of winning swimming in his brain, Ralph bounded into the kitchen and saw his sister, Phebe. She smiled at him, "Howdy, Ralph."

He grinned back at her and sat down next to her at the counter. "Morning, Phebe. How was your horse camp yesterday?" Phebe's eyes lit up. "It was the best day so far. Yesterday was show jumping day. We got to braid the tails of our horses and show off all the jumping skills that the camp had taught us. A funny thing happened, too. We had a girl show up with a mule, not a horse.

I didn't know that mules did show jumping, but this one did. He looked funny with his long pointed ears. But he did a good job on the course." While she was talking, Ralph grabbed a bowl and a spoon. "That sounds funny. Could you like mules as much as you like horses?" Phebe's eyes became a bit misty thinking about how much she adored horses, "No, horses will forever be my first choice.

Speaking of horses, I had better get finished packing my gear up. Miss Murphy told us to get there a little before eight o'clock so that we could finish grooming our horses." She reached down to pet George. Then she took her bowl over to the sink to rinse. Ralph looked at the clock and saw that it was getting close to time to go. He scooped oatmeal into his bowl, poured milk and honey on top and dug in.

While he was eating, he packed his lunch of a turkey sandwich, a yellow pear and a bottle of lemonade. His mom came down the stairs wearing her scrubs. She was going to the hospital after she dropped off Ralph and Phebe. "All right, slow poke. Time to get going. Have you brushed your teeth?" Ralph frowned. Of all days, he could not be late today. "Not yet. I'll be out in the car in five."

Ralph sprinted up the stairs, quickly brushed his teeth and grabbed his backpack. Going down the stairs he paused for a second to pat George on his back and then ran out the door. Phebe was in the car with their mom. Ralph jumped in and buckled his seat belt. His mom set off down the road. The farm where Phebe rode horses was near their house, so his mom drove there first.

When she drove into the parking lot, Miss Murphy was waiting at the entrance. Phebe jumped out of the car. Their mom told her, "Have a good time at camp today." Phebe waved for just a moment and then sprinted off to see her horse. Ralph grinned and told his mom, "Boy, mom. Phebe really likes horses."

404

His mom smiled, "Yes, she has since she was a little girl. It is so adorable." Switching subjects his mom asked him, "So, have you liked your camp so far?" Ralph smiled, "Yes, this is my best camp ever. I can't wait until we get there. Can you hurry?" "Well, Ralph, I really can't drive any faster. But it really isn't that far from here. And besides, you don't need to be there before nine o'clock." His mom was right.

It wasn't long before she drove into the parking lot for Skyline Park, where the camp was being held. Ralph got out of the car, waved to his mom and ran over to where his team, the Phantom Bears, was standing. One of their camp leaders, Joseph, was wearing a bright yellow shirt with their name Phantom Bears written on the back. When he saw Ralph he waved and told him, "Ralph, good that you are here.

I bought shirts with our team name on it for everyone." Ralph smiled, "That was good. Now we can all know where our team members are at during the Challenge." He slipped the new yellow shirt on over his white one. It wasn't long before all the rest of his team showed up. When everyone was there, their camp leaders told the kids to gather around the benches near the parking lot. When the kids had gathered there, Mister Phillips stood up.

Mister Phillips was in charge of Camp Skyline. "Boys and girls, today is going to be the best day of the week. Today, we are going to have our Grand Camp Challenge. As your team leaders may have told you, we will have two teams vying for the Camp Trophy. We will have three events. The team that wins at least two of the events will win the Camp Trophy." The campers all cheered.

Mister Phillips went on, "Let me tell you about the events. The first event is going to be a ropes course. Your job, as a team, is to get every member of your team to the finish line first. This is going to require effort by everyone on your whole team. Let's get going!" Both teams cheered. Everybody went down to where the ropes course was set up. When Ralph got there he went to stand next to his teammate, Miguel.

Joseph got the Phantom Bears together and told them, "There are four times during the course that you will need a partner to get past it. So I think that we should split up into pairs." One of Ralph's teammates, Miguel, spoke up, "That sounds like a good plan. How should we pair off?" Another teammate, Clare, offered her plan, "How about having us pair up by standing in a line and counting off odds and evens?

That way it will be fair and no one will get their feelings hurt." Their camp leader, Joseph, nodded, "That could be a good plan. Any others?" Ralph frowned. He did not like Clare's plan. Getting every one past the ropes course was going to be hard. It would be best if all their teammates could pair up based upon how much each camper could help their partner and not just care only about preventing hurt feelings.

So then, Ralph spoke up, "We could split up that way, but I think that we would be better to pair up based upon ability, not fairness. For example, we could have our strongest teammates pair up with the weakest ones." Clare frowned and shouted at Ralph, "That is going to make everyone feel badly. How would we pick the strongest and weakest?" Their team leader,

Joseph, frowned, "Clare, you can't shout at Ralph like that. Even if you don't like his plan. That is not polite. And his might be a good plan. Maybe if we have everyone sort themselves, then we could avoid those hurt feelings. And this might help us to get everyone across quickly. So let's try to line up. If you feel the most confident about the ropes course, you should stand here." He pointed to a spot next to a short olive tree.

Joseph went on, "And if you are not confident about the ropes course, you should stand next to the tall oak tree. Everyone else should try to line up between them." Jean was the first to go stand next to the olive tree. She was a good athlete and outstanding at ropes. It was her best sport and she felt good about mastering this course. Another girl, Ann, did not feel confident about the ropes course.

She felt tense and edgy looking at the ropes. She went to stand by the tall oak tree. It was not long before all of the Phantom Bears had lined up. Joseph smiled, "This looks good. Now, let's pair up starting with Jean and Ann. That way we can get our whole team across the ropes quickly. The other team, the Massive Elephants, had paired up differently. Three of the Massive Elephant pairs looked uneasy.

Ralph hoped that his plan would help his team to win. Mister Phillips called everyone to the starting line, "All right. Both teams, are you set?" Both teams shouted, "Yes!" Mister Phillips smiled. "Then let's go." The Massive Elephants got off to a good start. The first pair to go was Kevin and Madge. Both kids enjoyed the ropes course and went a lot faster than Jean and Ann.

Ann was feeling uneasy, but Jean helped her get across by showing her how to handle the ropes. Ralph started feeling uneasy. If his team lost then it would be his fault. He hoped that his plan would help them win. But now, after seeing the Massive Elephants get such a large lead, he was not confident that his team would win. The Massive Elephants all cheered when Kevin and Madge got to the other side first.

Ralph became even more tense when he saw more and more of the Massive Elephant pairs reaching the other side of the ropes course. But when it got down to the last three pairs, everything switched. The last three pairs of the Massive Elephants did not feel comfortable on the ropes. Even with their teammates trying to guide them, Don and Lee did not know how to get across the ropes.

Two pairs from the Phantom Bears passed them. Ralph started thinking that his team might catch up. When Don and Lee had reached the end, four pairs of Phantom Bears had passed them. Only two pairs remained for each team. The Phantom Bears that were left hustled up the ropes faster than the Massive Elephants. The Phantom Bears passed the struggling pair and won the event. Ralph was so happy. His plan had helped them all.

After the ropes challenge, it was time for lunch. On the way back to the picnic benches, Clare caught up to Ralph to walk with him. She told him, "Ralph, excuse me for snapping at you before the ropes course. I should not have yelled at you like that. Your plan really helped us all. It was fantastic!" Ralph smiled. It felt good to have won the first challenge.

After lunch, the two teams went down to the garden to hear about the second challenge. Mister Philips stood up and spoke to all the campers, "All right, campers. You did well on the ropes course. Congrats to the Phantom Bears for winning that challenge. But this next challenge will be quite difficult. I hope you are all set."

Mister Phillips pointed to a stack of large white cubes next to two tall poles, each with a flag on top. One flag was purple and the other was orange. "The next challenge is to take those large cubes and stack them so that you can get to the flag. The first team to get their flag down off the pole wins this challenge. You will have to be careful. The wood chips under the pole are not flat and might cause the cubes to tip or fall.

But if you fall, the wood chips will make a soft landing." He smiled and added, "But it might not be a good plan to try and fall." After Mister Phillips finished speaking, Joseph called the Phantom Bears over, "All right, guys. How should we take on this challenge?" Miguel spoke up first, "Those cubes don't look too difficult. We can stack them like a brick wall and have Jean go up to the top to get the flag."

Clare frowned, "But Miguel, those wood chips are going to make this difficult. Brick walls need a good base. How are we going to prevent the cubes falling down?" Miguel smiled, "If we are careful, we can stack them in a way that keeps them still." Ralph looked up at the pole. It didn't look too high. But it might take a long time to stack the cubes well. He spoke up, "I think that stacking them like a wall is going to take too long.

I think that we should take a chance and just set them next to each other and jump from one to the other to get to the top. That way we can get there quickly and win." Miguel looked at Ralph and smiled, too. "Ralph had a good plan last time. I vote to follow his plan this time too." Clare frowned, "But, Ralph, the wood chips will make it too difficult. The cubes will fall down and we will fail."

Ralph looked at Clare, "Clare, you could be wrong. If we had used your plan last time we would not have won. We won because of my plan. I think that we should follow my plan this time, too." All the other kids agreed and shouted, "Let's follow Ralph's plan." Clare looked upset but did not yell at Ralph this time. Then Joseph spoke, "All right, it looks like Ralph's plan is on."

The Phantom Bears went to stand next to the wood chips to start the second challenge. Mister Phillips raised his hand. "All right, teams. We are about to start our second challenge. On your marks. Get set." He paused looked around and then shouted, "Go!" Both teams sprinted for their cubes. The Massive Elephants started clearing the wood chips away from the base of the pole. The Phantom Bears started setting the cubes around the pole.

The Phantom Bears had the first row of cubes before the Massive Elephants had cleared the wood chips away. Ralph smiled. He was happy that his team was winning. Both teams stacked their cubes quickly. By the time the Phantom Bears had stacked up five layers of cubes, the Massive Elephants had only gotten three layers. After the sixth layer, Jean started going up the cubes to get their purple flag.

It looked like the Phantom Bears could really win this challenge, too. On the fourth layer, the cubes under Jean started to wobble. And then the cubes started to tilt. Jean tried to hustle up to the top of the stack and grab the flag but disaster occurred. The cubes all fell down. Jean fell with the cubes. She was not hurt because the wood chips padded her fall. But she was upset that she had not gotten the flag.

And the top three layers of cubes had fallen with her. The Phantom Bears all tried to stack up the cubes quickly, but the Massive Elephants had too large of a lead. One of the Massive Elephants, Raul, went up their stacked cubes to get the orange flag. The cube wall that the Massive Elephants had stacked did not wobble or fall. Clearing the wood chips away from the bottom of their cubes had helped keep them from falling.

Raul grabbed the orange flag from the top of the pole and yelled. The Massive Elephants all cheered. Ralph felt upset and disappointed. He had hoped that his plan would get to the flag first. But it had not. Clare frowned at Ralph, "We should have cleared the wood chips first, like I told you to. You should have used my plan!" She stomped off, mad at Ralph. Ralph felt horrible. He thought that she might be right.

If the Phantom Bears had cleared the wood chips before stacking the cubes then his team might have won. By telling everyone to ignore Clare, Ralph had made a big mistake. Joseph called the Phantom Bears together. Everyone on the team was sad. Joseph smiled, "I know that everyone is upset. But it is okay. We still have one more challenge, where we can make up for our loss. We can still win the trophy.

We need to meet down next to the lake for the next challenge. Let's go down there now." The whole team trudged down path, crossed a wooden bridge and ended up near the lake. Mister Phillips was there, standing on the wood dock jutting out into the lake. Two large row boats floated in the lake. One was yellow. The other was blue.

When both teams had arrived, Mister Phillips cleared his throat and spoke loudly, "The third and last challenge is a relay. Your teams need to row the boats across the lake to the boat house and back ten times." Ralph whispered to Miguel, "That is a long way, Miguel." Miguel nodded. He thought so, too. Mister Phillips went on, "You can trade rowers at this dock or at the boat house.

Or you can keep the same rowers in the boat all the way. That is up to you and your teammates. But to win this challenge, the most important thing is to get your row boat back here first. The Phantom Bears will be rowing in the yellow boat. And the Massive Elephants will row the blue one. Get organized and then we can start. It might take a while to plan and then walk over to the boat house.

If you need more time let me know. Otherwise we will start at three o'clock." Joseph called **the** Phantom Bears over **to** where he **was** standing. He started off by saying, "All right, Bears. This is our last challenge. How should we split up **the** rowing?" Clare had a plan, "I think that we should have our best rowers take **the** boat **the** whole way. That way we will not have **to** slow down **to** trade rowers.

437

It is rather long, but Jean and Ray are strong. It will be faster to have our strongest rowers going the whole time." Ralph looked at Clare. He disagreed, "Clare, no matter how strong Jean and Ray are, it is still too far for two rowers. I vote that we split the team up and have everyone take a turn rowing." Three of the other kids cheered Ralph's plan. Clare frowned, "Ralph, we did it your way last time and it failed.

You don't know how to win this. If we switch rowers, we will be too slow. We need to keep the same rowers the whole way." Ralph grew mad at hearing Clare. It was mean of her to say that. Ralph yelled, "Clare, That is wrong and unfair. I had a fantastic plan for our first challenge. We got unlucky with the cubes. I still know how to win this one."

Clare grimaced. She did not agree with Ralph. Joseph frowned at Ralph, "Ralph, you can't yell at Clare like that. We need to be polite and thoughtful." Ralph nodded, trying to cool himself down. Joseph was right. There was no need to shout at Clare. Ralph paused and thought about the problem. Maybe there was another way that used the best of both Clare's plan and his own.

Then Ralph had it. "Clare, how about we use both of our plans. That is, we can start with our best rowers and have back-up rowers if one or the other gets tired. How about that?" Clare thought for a moment and then she smiled, "Ralph, I think that that might be better. Part your plan and part mine." Ralph grinned, All the other teammates agreed. Part of the team walked down to the boat house.

Jean and Ray stayed on the dock to start the relay. At the start of the relay, Mister Phillips shouted, "Go!" and the boats started rowing across the lake. The Massive Elephants started with two strong rowers as well. Both boats rowed quickly and reached the other side at the same time. The Massive Elephants switched rowers. It slowed them down. Jean and Ray turned around and rowed quickly to get in front of the other team.

Ralph smiled. Jean and Ray got out on the other side and Miguel and Clare got in. The Massive Elephants switched their rowers there too. Miguel and Clare rowed quickly and got to the boat house. The Massive Elephants switched rowers one more time, slowing them down. The boats went back and forth across the lake. The Phantom Bears stayed in front of the other boat, winning the relay. Ralph was thrilled.

All **the** Phantom Bears started cheering. Clare gave Miguel a high five and jumped up and down. Clare turned and saw Ralph. She went over **to** him and told him, "Ralph, our plan helped us win. I am glad that we talked it out." Ralph smiled, "We make a good team, Clare." Ralph **was** still grinning when Mister Phillips announced that **the** Phantom Bears had won **the** trophy for **the** Grand Camp Challenge.

Mister Phillips handed out the baskets with the cool camping gear to all the Phantom Bears. Ralph carefully opened his basket and got out a carving knife. He couldn't wait to use it to make a walking stick. It wasn't long before Camp Skyline was over. Ralph's mom picked him up. She saw his trophy and smiled, "So Ralph, how did it go?" Ralph grinned, "Mom, we won! It was so cool. This was the best summer camp ever!"

The End

More Information on **SoundBlendS...**

Frequently Asked Questions

How fast should I go through the book?

A good pace is reading one story a week. The stories can be read a little bit each day or all in one sitting.

Sounding out the words seems slow.

Blending Sounds to form Words can seem very slow but this Reading Process is the fastest way to learn to decode! The goal of these stories is to facilitate the Sound-to-Print connection. Be patient. The end result will be wonderful.

Should the reader understand the stories?

A high degree of fluency is needed before the readers will be able to remember the sentences. Fluency is not expected during this program. Reading fluency is a characteristic that needs to be developed after the Sound-to-Print connection has been firmly established. Re-reading the sentences by the teacher (or parent) can be used to help with reading comprehension.

Why are there so few Sight Words?

It is the Sound-to-Print connection that is required to become a fluent reader. Teaching that Words should be memorized by their shape can confuse the reader about the Reading Process → connecting the Letters on the page with the Sounds in the Words.

Frequently Asked Questions

How is SoundBlendS different from Phonics?

In many Phonics programs, not all the Sounds are taught and there can be very little practice in Blending the Sounds to form Words. And there are very few stories that are available that do not make extensive use of Sight Words. SoundBlendS teaches all the Sounds and how to recognize the Letters that represent those Sounds. The Reading Process is obvious and simple for the beginning reader.

Why is reading English so complicated?

English spelling has a long history. It would be easier to teach reading if there was only one symbol (Letter) for each Sound. Several features (using multiple letters for one Sound and using those same letters for more than one Sound) in English spelling do complicate the reading process. SoundBlendS was developed to make these features obvious and simple to the beginning reader.

When should learning the letter names start?

Letter names are essential for Spelling. Teaching Letter Names can usually start after Letter Groups are introduced (Story 7).

Letter Names

Letters	Letter Names
• A a	• Ay
• B b	• Bee
• C c	• See
• D d	• Dee
• E e	• Ee
• F f	• Eff
• G g	• Jee
• H h	• Aych
• I i	• Igh
• J j	• Jay
• K k	• Kay
• L l	• Ell
• M m	• Emm

Letter Names

Letters	Letter Names
• N n	• Enn
• O o	• Oa
• P p	• Pee
• Q q	• Kyoo
• R r	• Ar
• S s	• Ess
• T t	• Tee
• U u	• Yoo
• V v	• Vee
• W w	• Dubul-Yoo
• X x	• Eks
• Y y	• Wigh
• Z z	• Zee

Vowel Sounds

	Sound	Spellings
	**a**nt	a
	**e**lephant	e ea ai
	**i**guana	i y ui
	**o**ctopus	o al a
	**u**mbrella	u o o_e ou

Vowel Sounds

	Sound	Spellings
	**jay**	a_e ai a ay ei eigh ey
	**ee**l	ea ee y ie ei ey e e_e
	**eye**	i_e ie i y igh eye
	b**oa**t	o_e o oa ow oe ou ough
	**u**nicorn	u_e u ew eu you

Vowel Sounds

	Sound	Spellings
	**h**aw**k**	aw au ough augh
	**m**oo**n**	oo ue ew u ou ui ough
	**b**oo**k**	oul oo u
	**ow**l	ou ow ough
	**oy**ster	oi oy

Vowel Sounds

	Sound	Spellings
	**ar**madillo	ar orr
	b**ir**d	er ur ir or ear ere urr
	**or**ca	or ore oar our oor
	b**ear**	are air arr err ear ere

Consonant Sounds

	Sound	Spellings
	**b**ee	b bb
	**c**at	c k ck ch cc q
	**d**og	d dd ed
	**f**ish	f ff ph gh
	**g**oat	g gg gh gu gue

Consonant Sounds

	Sound	Spellings
	horse	h wh
	jaguar	j g ge dge dg
	lion	l ll
	moose	m mm mb mn me
	newt	n nn gn kn ne

Consonant Sounds

	Sound	Spellings
	**p**anda	p pp
	**r**accoon	r rr wr rh
	**s**eal	s ss sc se c sw
	**t**iger	t tt bt ed th
	**v**iper	v ve

Consonant Sounds

	Sound	Spellings
	**w**olf	w wh
	fo**x**	x
	**y**ak	y
	**z**ebra	z zz ze se s x
	slo**th**	th the

Consonant Sounds

	Sound	Spellings
	**sh**ark	sh sch s
	**ch**icken	ch tch
	ri**ng**	ng
	trea**s**ure	s ss

Combination Sounds

	Sounds	Spellings
	**qu**ail	qu
	cas**tle**	le tle al el ol
	musi**cian**	tion sion cian
	deli**cious**	xious cious

Made in the USA
Columbia, SC
20 April 2021